"What would it mean to welcome that which haunts European theology, continental philosophy, and those of us who find meaning in these traditions? How would welcoming excluded realities and ideas unsettle stabilized identities and norms? Wrestling with hauntings of the understandings of the self and world he continues to find meaningful, Colby Dickinson offers an honest and challenging political-theological reflection. This timely book makes a significant contribution to political theology and continental philosophy for both students and scholars."

—JOSEPH DREXLER-DREIS,
associate professor of theology, Xavier University of Louisiana

"This is a book that I have been waiting for Colby Dickinson to publish: a comprehensive, accessible overview of his philosophy and theology. Whether you are new to his work or have been following the development of Dickinson's thought throughout the years, this poignant, expressive, and deeply sincere book delivers on all fronts."

—JUSTIN SANDS,
research fellow, University of the Free State

"This book is wonderful. Colby Dickinson faces continental philosophical and theological traditions that formed him, but that also haunt him. Allied to thinkers that promote a turn regarding that tradition, an overture to interpretative forms of minorities and those from the Global South is unveiled. By contrasting hetero-biography to autobiography, he finds vigor to disempower sovereignty in its excluding structure. Refined literarily and conceptually, this work is very welcomed and necessary in times of extremism."

—GLAUCO BARSALINI,
professor of religious studies, Pontifical Catholic University of Campinas

D1697981

Haunted Words, Haunted Selves

Haunted Words, Haunted Selves

Listening to Otherness within Western Thought

COLBY DICKINSON

CASCADE *Books* · Eugene, Oregon

HAUNTED WORDS, HAUNTED SELVES
Listening to Otherness within Western Thought

Cascade Books
An Imprint of Wipf and Stock Publishers
199 W. 8th Ave., Suite 3
Eugene, OR 97401

www.wipfandstock.com

PAPERBACK ISBN: 978-1-6667-6921-0
HARDCOVER ISBN: 978-1-6667-6922-7
EBOOK ISBN: 978-1-6667-6923-4

Cataloguing-in-Publication data:

Names: Dickinson, Colby, author.

Title: Haunted words, haunted selves : listening to otherness within western
thought / Colby Dickinson.

Description: Eugene, OR : Cascade Books, 2024 | Includes bibliographical
references and index.

Identifiers: ISBN 978-1-6667-6921-0 (paperback) | ISBN 978-1-6667-6922-7
(hardcover) | ISBN 978-1-6667-6923-4 (ebook)

Subjects: LCSH: Other (Philosophy). | Postcolonialism. | Continental
philosophy. | Philosophical theology.

Classification: BT40 .D52 2024 (paperback) | BT40 .D52 (ebook)

03/20/24

Contents

Acknowledgments

PARTS OF THE INTRODUCTION were originally presented at a talk given on ghosts at Loyola University Chicago in 2012. Many thanks to Aana Vigen for the invitation to give this talk and all of my wonderful colleagues there who attended, but also who have been so incredibly supportive of various parts of this research. For all the great conversations over the years, I want to thank Bret Lewis, Mara Brecht, Chris Skinner, Aana Vigen, Josefrayn Sanchez-Perry, Hugh Nicholson, Emily Cain, Hille Haker, John McCarthy, Susan Ross, Bob DiVito, Xueying Wang, Olivia Stewart Lester, Mark Lester, Edmondo Lupieri, Miguel Diaz, Devorah Schoenfeld, Yarina Liston, Teresa Calpino, Lauren O'Connell, Bill French, Tom Wetzel, and Jon Nilson.

Chapter 1 was originally a lecture delivered at Marquette University for a colloquium on narrative approaches to the self at the Center for the Advancement of the Humanities in April 2022. Many thanks to Ethan Vanderleek for the invitation, and to Jorge Montiel, Mariana Ortega, and Dan McAdams, and the many colloquium participants for the wonderful conversations there.

A small section of chapter 1 was first published as "Whose Fetish? A Response to Prof. J. Lorand Matory, Author of *The Fetish Revisited: Marx, Freud, and the Gods Black People Make*," *The Religious Studies Project*, October 5, 2020. https://www.religiousstudiesproject.com/response/whose-fetish/.

I owe a major debt to Justin Sands, for suggesting that I try to write a book like this one. It was his challenge that brought the current book into existence, and I am very grateful for his prodding to produce this work.

Many thanks are also due to Whitney Harper and Jack Nuelle for their fine editing and formatting skills.

Preface

IT SEEMS AS IF everyone I know who reads my work says to me at some point something like: "Hey, you should try writing about what you do, but for ordinary people." I usually agree, but then find it difficult to write something in such a simple, direct way. My books have generally been dense academic exercises in philosophical and theological thinking. There is a rigor and language appropriate to each discipline that, in some ways, has to be respected. At the same time, my teaching has been straightforward and often in extremely plain terms, as I try to interest and excite students who have little background in formal, academic disciplines.

I realized at some point that when I am teaching, and I simplify my thoughts in order to speak directly to students in a way that they will understand, I am also synthesizing all of my writing. This is, however, something I have so far refrained from doing in my writing.

All of my writing has been produced without the demand of an audience for completion; I was finishing my thoughts in class, with students, in an abridged form and with clear and direct application and theses, which were subsequently missing in the books I wrote. I left all this out of my writing, which has a more scholarly and academic tone.

A friend of mine, however, recently challenged me to write a short book that takes all of my published writing into account and tries to tie it all together, offering insight into the large, sprawling body of work I have thus far fashioned. I accepted his challenge enthusiastically, as I knew that this task remained yet to be demonstrated, even and especially to myself.

This book is in many ways an attempt to reckon with what has haunted my thought, and all of my writing, but what I have not been able to say directly and in a concise manner. The issues that I have been reflecting on throughout this short and not entirely elegant book arrived on my desktop throughout the years as I immersed myself further and further in the philosophical, theological, and literary worlds that I inhabit from time to time.

These are worlds, mind you, that I also inherited to some degree and which I sought to explore the limits of throughout my writing.

It is no surprise that most of what I have dealt with has been firmly western in its orientation, mostly Christian, and more often than not involving straight white male authors. In case there was any doubt about the Eurocentric nature of what I do, the tradition of philosophy that I follow closely is called "continental philosophy" by those who practice it—a reference to the only continent that would dare see itself as the only one not needing to be named distinctly. It's like being asked what country I come from and saying that I hail from *the* country, which is pretty much what the more arrogant citizens of these United States are probably thinking anyway. My point is that not a lot of humility generated through self-critical awareness is generally present in such exercises.

I enjoy what I research, study, and write about, and I won't soon be leaving the field of so-called continental philosophy behind. When you acquire an expertise in something because you have a passion for it, you tend to stick with it for the long haul. This being said, I have to confess that the lack of a true comparative understanding of our world's many philosophies is not just startling, it is a product of the colonialist, imperialist, racist, and sexist legacies that have permeated the West for centuries.

Sure, I found my academic love because of the background I came from. Being raised Protestant in the state of Illinois, in a county with near zero racial or ethnic diversity, the classics of western thought appealed to me immediately as a bit of "my story" written by "my ancestors" in some sense. After working through so many texts and having written so many books and hopefully having deepened my understanding of many issues that I had no idea were so complex and so enriching to discuss, I still find myself saying (mostly to myself, but now to you): You know, maybe some ancient Chinese philosophers had a better grasp of a particular ethical issue than either Plato or Aristotle did. Or, perhaps we might get further as a nation utilizing the African political philosophy of ubuntu rather than looking once again to Hobbes's theory of human nature. Or, perhaps posed as a question to myself, what indigenous ideas on the environment offer better approaches to human stewardship than this capitalistic mess we have gotten ourselves into?

As someone who has worked in the past within Christian theological circles that are oblivious to any other religious tradition's teachings and how such teachings, if learned properly and respectfully, might yield some pretty good insights on the religious nature of the human being, I find it sad, *tragic* in fact, that we are still peddling particular worldviews that are willfully ignorant of the rich diversity of peoples and traditions that surround us every day.

Once in a while, I find a colleague or peer lost in wonderment when they finally do take notice of a tradition well outside of their own, and the insights it contains, but most of the academics I know spend too much of their time feeling like secret frauds because there is just so much that they *don't* know, even about the topics on which they are so-called experts. I suppose it's hard to learn about something completely foreign to you when you are too busy feeling insecure about your own identity. Or maybe that's precisely when someone *should* dive into something wholly unknown to them, for it might have the power to shake up their world for the better.

Sometimes I find myself reminding my students that humanity has really only been attempting interreligious dialogue for somewhere around fifty years, so we really don't have a clue yet about how the recognition of all this plurality will alter the course of humanity (though the fact that our youth are mainly dropping religion altogether and starting to ask questions about the rampant nonsense that previous generations have been up to is a pretty good sign of what's to come). Then I look at the way in which certain philosophy departments haven't typically recognized non-western philosophical traditions as what they should be teaching, and I know we still have a long way to go.

This book is my attempt to tie up some loose ends within my own field, pointing all the while toward horizons of conversation that have yet to be taken up more fully. It is therefore a book about being haunted by that which we have neglected, but which haunts us nonetheless, asking us to take notice and to consider life from a point of view we had previously refused to welcome.

Introduction

WE ARE ALL HAUNTED by something, perhaps something we know all-too-well but fear, or something we have repressed deep within so as to not have to face it, or maybe by something we have no conscious knowledge of, but which we flee from in terror nonetheless.

Every place we inhabit is a place already inhabited.[1] Every building, every land, is already filled—or *over*filled—with so many presences that came there before us, whether we chose to acknowledge this reality or not. These presences living among us unseen are unconsciously at work in our representations of our lands, our houses, and even ourselves.

There are so many presences, interacting in such complex ways, that we are often not able to comprehend the vast networks of relations of which we are a part. We often have to reduce or restrict our representations of things, persons, and events in order to make sense of our world, reducing much fuller realities so that we might reach a shared understanding of some kind.

For this reason, much of what we deal with in our lives is often removed from our immediate reality, or our *seeing*. It is quite simply forgotten.[2] Taking the time to deal with the various things we have repressed, both in a historical sociocultural sense and on a personal level, constitutes a study in its own right, one perhaps psychological or *hauntological*, as the French philosopher Jacques Derrida once put it.[3]

The various social injustices humanity has historically faced (e.g., racial, gendered, class inequalities and oppressions, and so forth) are therefore immediately implicated within such a framework of the haunted.[4] Like

1. This point is articulated well in Butler, *Parting Ways*.

2. On the processes of memory involved in constructing a workable version of the self, see Ricoeur, *Memory, History, Forgetting*.

3. Derrida, *Specters of Marx*. His view of messianicity as a structural form of the repressed returning, or the revenant, makes sense only within such a hauntological understanding.

4. Gordon, *Ghostly Matters*. The sociological focus taken up by Gordon is explicitly also furthered in Hill, *Paranormal Media*.

Toni Morrison's character Sethe is haunted by the ghost "Beloved," we are haunted by our crimes, by humanity's crimes, by our own inhumanity, indeed the inhumanity that *comprises* our humanity.

There's an old stand-up comedy routine that has been done by both Richard Pryor and Eddie Murphy, each invoking the same punchline. Essentially, the joke turns on the fact that most movies about haunted houses involve white people trying to stay in their homes, protect their property, and to fight the ghosts that haunt them, whereas black people hear strange voices telling them to get out and they immediately leave the scene, not waiting a minute to see what presence lurks there. It's the white people who try to possess the haunted house itself, to conquer, control, suppress, or repress their ghosts, which they may have themselves created, whereas the black people have no business there, have nothing to prove or maybe to "fight for" in this sense, in order to possess what came before them.

What is the truth of the joke, as Freud would have it? White people have many ghosts with which they wrestle. Black people, though they may have any number of ghosts haunting them—such as the myriad legacies of historical injustice—do not have the same cultural memory haunting them in this land as white people do. Neither do Native Americans, or First Nations, for that matter, for they are themselves a diverse group with a much more complex relationship to the spirits that preceded all of us, a relationship more respectful and generally aware of its standing with regard to everything else around them. It is one thing to be haunted by the traumas you are willing to recognize because you demand justice in relation to them; it is another thing to cover over such traumas as if they did not happen.

What is a ghost exactly? It is soul. It is spirit. It is an immaterial thing yet affiliated with "the principle of life," as the *Oxford English Dictionary* has it.

Gilbert Ryle, through his use of the phrase "ghost in the machine," referred to the activity of the mind—a thing we have historically had much trouble relating to the materiality of the body.[5] Our spirit, it would seem, has trouble being pinned down or located. Perhaps fittingly, then, as Thomas Hobbes made clear in one of the earliest uses of another sense of the word *ghost*, it is also an "idol" or "Phantasme of the Imagination."[6]

A spirit, of course, as with a ghost, is a specter or an apparition, that which seemingly appears of its own accord and beyond the normal rules which govern the principle of life. This would make some sense then as to

---

5. Ryle, *Concept of Mind*.

6. Hobbes, *Leviathan*, cited in the OED, iii. xxxiv. 208.

why our spirit, our essence, is not perceivable as it lies outside the principles which govern our bodies—yet it is perhaps in many ways no more than our bodies.

We can't even begin to think the separation of spirit from our material, bodily reality. Yet spirit seems almost undeniable in terms of its existence. This is our unexplainable essence, spirit, or soul that permeates our bodily being and is at once equated to, and often portrayed as superior to, our material selves. Spirits appear, like ghosts, as that unexplainable excess to materiality that we are unable to define.[7] This is probably the scariest thing we could say about our being-human: that something within us seems to exceed us.

So are there ghosts out there? What does it mean to say that we believe in them? Or, perhaps, more pointedly and informatively, what makes up our fear of ghosts? How do these disparate strands of intuitive (over)reaction motivate and drive us in all-too-human ways?

Understanding ourselves within a given context or spatial location means learning to see our ghosts. As Jeffrey Kripal has put it, understanding the role of the paranormal in our world is fundamentally a hermeneutical endeavor, because such a reading "encodes an approach to the paranormal as meaning and story and insists on the interpreter's creative role in the interpretation."[8]

Ghosts don't come from nowhere—they have a history, they are a history. They are "encoded" within a particular representational and deeply historical economy that *can* be understood. They may lie at the limits of such an economy's intelligibility, but they speak—albeit vaguely at times—*of* that economy's functioning.

As Kripal argues, "anomalies may also be the signals of the impossible, that is, signs of the end of one paradigm and the beginning of another."[9] One economy ends, and another is born, though what seemed at first to lay outside the bounds of our understanding eventually came to be considered as the norm, a new norm for a new order. This is the nature of thought itself, and what Kripal sees as a sure sign that the sacred—our way of typically designating the creation of such an order—will not simply go away in the secular age in which we live. We are haunted by the sacred, even as we try to live without any sense of it.

Such a vision, as he goes on to outline, is what allows us to envision the sacred as a category *within* the structure of consciousness itself, not simply

---

7. See the reflections of Santner, *On Creaturely Life.*
8. Kripal, *Authors of the Impossible*, 196.
9. Kripal, *Authors of the Impossible*, 253.

a stage along some progressive evolutionary path of human development.[10] "Fact or fraud, trick or truth, whatever paranormal phenomena are, they clearly vibrate at the origin point of many popular religious beliefs, practices, and images—from beliefs in the existence, immortality, and transmigration of the soul; through the felt presence of deities, demons, spirits, and ghosts; to the fearful fascinations of mythology and the efficacy of magical thinking and practice. But if the paranormal lies at the origin point of so much religious experience and expression, it should also lie at the center of any adequate theory of religion."[11]

From this angle, and despite the increasing loss of traditional forms of religious belief in the modern era, humanity cannot simply abandon our belief in ghosts or in religion; rather, we must understand how such structures of belief affect our understanding of ourselves. We are haunted for a reason, and we have to spend some time acquainting ourselves with just what that reason is.

As Julia Kristeva has put it, we have an incredible need to believe; yet what is it that we are believing in and why are we believing it?[12] What are we fleeing from in terror and what are we embracing? Our answers say as much about us as they do about what it is we are wanting to believe in.

Ever since I first read and admired Carl Sagan's *The Demon-Haunted World*, I have wondered in what ways I fail to see the demons that haunt my somewhat crowded world of various different figures, symbols, and representations.[13] I think of my work and my writing in particular, whether I pay attention to, or even *want* to pay attention to, certain unspoken or unthought elements within my innumerable worlds which, if listened to, might upend and redirect my work altogether.

The work I do needs to look at the ghosts I fear to confront, yet, by definition, there is so much that remains unseen and which haunts me. Striving for honesty in my work, however, means nothing less than seeking to listen to what haunts me, to wrestle with my own ghosts as humans have often claimed to wrestle with God. The problem, of course, is that we are often incapable of recognizing what haunts us in the first place, that it is there, that it exists and perhaps even seeks after us.

---

10. Kripal, *Authors of the Impossible*, 255.

11. Kripal, *Authors of the Impossible*, 253.

12. Kristeva, *This Incredible Need to Believe*.

13. Sagan, *Demon-Haunted World*. See also, Sagan, *Varieties of Scientific Experience*, as well as the general focus in Bridgstock, *Beyond Belief*.

Freud made it abundantly clear in his work that the more we ignore those things that we try to repress—in ourselves, in our communities, in our cultural memories, in our histories—the more those things come back to haunt us, seemingly with a vengeance. He called this the return of the repressed, and he tried to understand how ignoring those dark corners of our lives means that they will come back to haunt us as if they were fated to destroy us.

So many deep philosophical questions linger in this formulation of the human psyche: how do our ghosts strive to make peace with us, like those ghosts in M. Night Shyamalan's film *The Sixth Sense* (1999) who are just looking to be seen, to be recognized for the traumas they have suffered? Do we ever get rid of our ghosts or do they, in some sort of move that would make Hegelian dialectics proud, learn to live side-by-side with us, within us even, no longer repressed, but no longer secretly subverting the ways we try to present our identities?

For Freud, there were intriguing religious questions circulating around the return of the repressed. By his calculations, his own ancestral religion, Judaism, was most likely an ancient Egyptian religion once celebrated by the monotheistic pharaoh Ahkenaton, a sacred path that was later consciously repressed by a more official Egyptian polytheistic culture. Ahkenaton's memory was dramatically effaced from the cultural record, as Egyptian pharaohs tried to alter their own history. Yet, Freud speculated— and in ways that would drive historians crazy through his apparent lack of scientific rigor on the subject—Moses *the Egyptian* had brought back this repressed cult of Ahkenaton and took it to a new level, by rejecting the "false idols" of Egypt, taking a minority population to a new land, in effect creating a new *people* entirely and bringing into the light of day a new sense of divine being.[14]

Like so many minority populations within a given normative, nationalistic context, the Israelites embodied their oppression as *the* repressed element of Egyptian society, identifying with a repressed God and bringing that God's existence to light *so that* they might bring their own existence into being at the same time. Even if the historical evidence didn't yield a completely seamless account of what Freud conjectured, his theory made a lot of sense psychologically speaking.

Almost a hundred years later, we are still taking account of Freud's thesis and noticing how there is a certain truth in this profound ability to sculpt one's sense of self through an identification with the repressed elements of a given society, a religious culture, or a national politics.[15] When

14. Freud, *Moses and Monotheism*. See also Yerushalmi, *Freud's Moses*.
15. See Winter, *Freud and the Institution*.

we identify with the repressed element, a new way of being in the world opens to us, hopefully providing humanity with an opportunity for a more just representation of things to stand up and be recognized. Though such identifications are often taken to be subversions and disruptions of a normative order—which they very much are—we have to learn to see how the truth manifests itself more directly within such challenges.

For the postcolonial theorist Edward Said, Freud's notion of the return of the repressed was something that shed an important light on how a repressed element, according to Freud, was really an antinomian force. It was that which appeared to be opposed to all normative order, all law even, though it was a force that arose from within the normative order, not from outside of it.[16] This was a major insight to achieve. Recognizing the *internal* origin of such forces allows us to see how we can't blame some *external* other for the problems we encounter when our socially recognized, and so often privileged, identities fall apart.

We are haunted by ghosts because we *need* to be haunted by ghosts, so that we might begin to take notice of those things that we have been ignoring, so that the repressed elements of our world might have a chance to speak and so that we might allow more just representations of reality to ultimately appear.

Was darkness the thing we repressed so that we might construct a sacred sense of the light? Was goodness what was possible only by suppressing the "bad"? But what about the spirit or soul repressing the body, which may be in need of liberation? Or what about those dark shadows inside us—our dark shadows—that need to be heard so that they stop directing our conscious behaviors in ways that we can't help but notice on a daily basis?

Teaching high school religion classes on the Bible many years ago at a Catholic high school—Hebrew Scriptures in the fall semester, Christian Scriptures in the spring—I was constantly puzzled by the dualities that I encountered in the varied texts that comprised this vast library of ancient literature that people often mistakenly think of as a single "book." There were, of course, the classics, like God and the devil, good and evil, the righteous and the wicked, heaven and hell, death and resurrection, body and soul, God's will and human desire, old and new, light and dark, promise

16. Said, *Freud and the Non-European.*

and hypocrisy, order and chaos, male and female, Jew and gentile, as well as slave and free, to name just some of the many that seemed to appear on virtually every page of these scriptures.

To be more specific, I was fascinated by how these dualisms cropped up in nearly every major religious tradition across the globe, indicating that something larger was afoot, and I was bedeviled by the way in which these dualisms were not only the support beams of religious belief, but how they were not really analyzed for what they were, just taken for granted.

The natural way in which humans seem to just accept an "us" versus "them" dichotomy, without any problematic criticism arising, is more than just baffling—it's disturbing. I mean, what if I was born over there with "them" instead of here with "us," or, à la Romeo and Juliet, what if I fall in love with one of "them," or, even more disturbing, what if I engage some self-awareness and come to realize that an essential piece of what makes "them" appear as "them" to "us" is actually something deeply lodged within me as well?

I am constantly haunted by such thoughts, as I think we all should be.

Such a realization, many a psychologist will tell you, has the power to disable our sense of self as well as our sense of community (the "us" part). We might feel almost permanently adrift on some high, wavy seas if we even caught a glimpse of how what we hate most in our enemies might actually be a significant part of us as well. We might even hate our enemies so much *because* we are in denial about how similar we are to them.

This entire line of reasoning reminds me of the stories I used to read about in the news at the end of the last century where a major opponent of gay marriage suddenly realizes that he (because usually it was a "he") is actually himself gay, or at least "troubled" by his same-sex desire, as many evangelical Christians used to put it.

We might chuckle at the foibles of those living in denial of their own core desires, but the larger religious problem remains right before our eyes: what about all of those dualities that seem to structure our entire worldview, causing religious grandparents everywhere to shake their heads in holy despair when they hear that their young grandchild was engaging in some immoral, sinful behavior clearly needing to be labeled as evil or heathen or godless so that their progeny's progeny might come back into the safety of the fold?

We use dualistic ways of structuring our world because we have a strong desire to impose order upon everything so that we might not only understand reality, but somehow also control it. To name something is, in some ways, to control it and so to have a certain power over our fears of it. From Adam's naming of the animals to our parents yelling our full names at us when we are in trouble, something about these reductive labels brings us a sense of comfort and control at the same time.

Order and control come about easily—and what will always appear in retrospect to be "naturally" too, though it is often anything but "natural"— through the fabrication of a duality that favors one side over another, such as with male and female, strong and weak, and us and them, to name but a few more prominent dualistic ways of dividing up our world. Religiously, separations between the orthodox and heretics, as between transcendence and immanence, or grace and nature, become pronounced features of communal identity so that the necessary illusions that divide our world, such as with us/them or intimate/stranger, become projected onto a scale with cosmic proportions (e.g., heaven and hell, the saved and the damned).

Every act of separating the world into such dualistic frameworks, however, means that we will constantly be haunted by the "other" side of things, unable to let go of how the division itself seems to speak of a prior wholeness and complexity that was abandoned so that we might master both ourselves and others.

Myths spin dualistic cosmologies that structure potentially every detail of a person's life, providing comfort, consolation, and consistency when we most need it. Though these myths and their accompanying dualisms are ultimately our imaginative creations, they are nonetheless necessary illusions that we cannot do without. We need our identities in order to recognize a shared set of symbols and so as well to understand one another.

Even though such illusions are subject to being criticized, taken apart, and ultimately refashioned completely, they are still what we must bear in order to access any form of communication with one another.

Though modern culture often wishes to act as if it has removed premodern dualities from its logic, such as one readily locates in the many folklores and religions of the world—nature/grace, male/female, good/evil—the modern self is beset by just as many dualities that structure our lives almost without exception. From the subject/object and mind/body divisions to arguments about nature versus culture, from discussions of closed and open societies as well as conscious and unconscious desires to the partisan rhetoric of the left and the right, we are thoroughly immersed in mythological dualities despite our best efforts to critically disabuse ourselves of the enchanted in favor of a disenchanted ("enlightened") perspective.

We believe we have removed the sacred from our world and then we are haunted by the desire within us for faith in that which exceeds us.

Philosophically in the West, we continue to debate the same dualisms that have structured our thoughts for centuries: form and content, the One and the many, the beautiful and the ugly, infinite and finite, memory and forgetting, love and hate, illusion and reality. Philosophy functions for human reasoning in this way much as theology has functioned for politics—to bolster and support the practical aspects of life with a rich theoretical underpinning. The king's right to rule was often perceived as divinely mandated, just as our logics are lined with philosophical arguments for why we work the way we do, even if we don't completely understand the ins and outs of how our rationalities are put together.

Metaphysics, in this sense, has generally existed as a series of abstract theoretical formulations about the nature of God and other abstract "god stuff" that typically justifies the political markers and divisions of our world. From sovereign powers to gendered norms, humankind likes to arrange matters so that they appear as if God made reality the way we have shaped it with our own hands, and then we freak out when we see another human, or group of humans, trying to refashion reality into a more equitable shape.

The first thing I would note to my students back when I taught high school was that most of the terms on either side of the dualism were more than a bit problematic. Trying to defend a dualistic reference to God versus Satan, for example, was never so simple—and not just because Satan was always an extremely vague literary character.

In an ancient Hebrew context, "God" could be understood from a variety of different perspectives. There was "El," the mightiest of mighty ones who was more than just a Hebrew God, and actually belonged to other traditions in the area as well, complete with various mythologies—some of which also made it into the Bible. For example, El traditionally had a wife named Asherah, but she was cut out of this upstart monotheism because there could only be one God, though the Israelites, especially the women, had trouble understanding that Asherah wasn't part of a package deal.

Then there was YHWH, or Yahweh, of whom the Jews don't pronounce the name, but whom Christians embraced with Latin flair, eventually updating it to the transliterated "Jehovah."

Then there was the always clever Elohim, which is actually a plural noun for "the gods," meaning that the singular deity was, at times, referred to in the plural. Christians might claim that this was an early reference to the Trinity, but that was clearly not what was going on here. Perhaps God was using some "royal we" type reference, or perhaps there was a polytheism at the center of God's monotheistic being, arguably as in India.

In Christianity, things get much more complex, and quickly, as an embodied God in the form of Jesus, alongside a spirit manifest as a dove and sometimes called the Holy Ghost, kind of turn the whole singular God thing on its head, as Christianity's critics might be happy to point out.

My point here is that whatever we westerners call God isn't always so clear. It's so unclear, in fact, that trying to produce a central protagonist in opposition to an evil demiurge is nigh impossible. For many, it isn't entirely clear that the terrible things that happen in our world aren't actually *caused by* God, or God's will.

My students quickly discovered that trying to construct a unified and singular image of God—and so also unassailable and reinforced against any perceived criticism—always leads inevitably to a crisis in God's legitimacy, or what we call the problem of theodicy. If God is all-powerful and all-knowing, then why do bad things happen to good people?

It would be fair to say that this question perpetually haunts a good many believers.

This question is really a question about the construct of God that many people have formed. In other words, the problem isn't why bad things happen to good people—because they do happen, all the time, and such things have less to do with God than with other people, who use violence or cause accidents, etc.—but why someone was trying to come up with an image of a deity that was so all-powerful in the first place. The sign that we haven't yet learned this lesson can be found in how many people, even today, want to blame the elected leaders of their country for things that have nothing to do with their elected position or political role.

Regarding the dualism of God and Satan, things don't fare much better. The first reference to Satan in the Bible is actually to what most translators have called an angel who just happens to play the oppositional role to the prophet Balaam who is trying to sneak away from a divine mandate. This is our first clue that something is amiss in our understanding of the devil, whose title, including the direct article preceding it, alerts us to the fact that this figure was originally conceived as more of a position than a person, like "the police officer" or "the fire fighter." The Satan, then, was any angelic being who literally played the role of the "devil's advocate" to God's opinions, as we witness in the Book of Job where God seems to be playing fast and loose with the life of one of his faithfully devoted.

Satan actually developed slowly over time to become something of an embodiment of all those evils that we dare not look at too closely. Satan, that is, became a fabrication intended to stand in for all those other gods and idols that were tempting the Israelites away from monotheism.

But, for many religious persons, the devil haunts us, threatening to destroy or delegitimate our good sense of self and the world we inhabit. Perhaps the Satan haunts us for a reason, though, as a source of permanent challenge to whatever life we have constructed for ourselves.

What really blew my mind, though, weren't just the fundamental antagonisms that painted an "us-versus-them" mentality, which remained relatively unexamined throughout history. These dualisms are, quite simply, the common backdrop against which so many oppositions are not-so-cleverly struck: the hometown good guys versus the out of town, much disparaged, "backwards" foreigners.

What struck me as more than a bit significant was the way in which there seemed to be an internal divide within the theologies of Israel that was going almost unrecognized at times, what I came to call the tension between the prophetic and the legalistic sides of ancient Judaism. Here was a subtle duality that did not always rise to the level of an us versus them, but rather seemed to be active at an almost subconscious level *within* the sense of an "us" that structured ancient biblical life.

This tension was so obvious, and so massive, but it went mostly unacknowledged throughout the Hebrew Scriptures. It just kind of appeared and no one really felt the need to directly confront it the way that one imagines the righteous faithful become compelled at times to slay the wickedly pagan.

But the prophets haunted the legalistically minded, and those stressing a legalistic outlook on faith haunted the prophets in a sense too.

So too, I wondered, why weren't the social justice minded prophets slaying the religious bureaucrats from time to time, or, conversely, why weren't community religious leaders locking up the prophets and throwing away the key? Or, more to the point, why didn't one side win the battle and cut the other side's views and texts out of the Bible altogether, as most victors have done throughout history? This would have been arguably the best way to give readers the solid impression that only one side existed from the origin of all creation, because that's how it's really done if you want people to fear the cohesive portrait of the Lord you are trying to present.

Instead, what we get are books like Ezra and Nehemiah where the laws are being read aloud to the people of Israel and the people are quaking in their sandals because they haven't followed the laws that God gave them. So, for example, when they hear that a good Israelite isn't supposed to marry a foreign, non-Jewish woman, we are told that they suddenly grab such women by the hair and drag them out of the community, symbolically and literally expelling them from life among the righteous.

And then we also get prophets who say wild things like "God cares nothing for your sacrifices and your rituals. You should stop trying to follow the laws so closely and start working harder to bring justice into the world," which seems like pretty much the opposite sentiment to the ethos that Ezra was working hard to create.[17]

If you feel like these two diametrically opposed philosophies eerily seem to echo our contemporary account of what divides a conservative from a liberal, you are not mistaken. In fact, I sometimes feel like I've spent the last decade simply trying to understand how this tension plays itself out in so many different domains, from political partisanship to philosophical argument.

On my own academic planet, this tension can be felt in the conflict between the philosophical communitarians, who defend the necessity of community, values, and identity often by reverting to the views of premodern writers, and those pesky postmodern deconstructionists who seem ill at ease with nearly every community value that exists, often trying to undermine the claims of tradition in order to promote greater justice for the marginalized members of the community.[18]

I have been part of faculties where the demonstrations of passive-aggressive tendencies between these two rival factions seemed to want to spill over at times into open hostility, ironically mirroring the way that many envision apocalyptic battles between good and evil, or even Democrats and Republicans in my own national context. I sometimes chuckle to myself when I see these tensions playing out in the academic world because most academics I know pretend as if they are highly enlightened creatures who would never be so base as to descend to the shenanigans and hijinks of politically partisan hackery, and yet here we are.

Recognizing how we are ceaselessly haunted by that which threatens to undo our representations of ourselves is more or less the point of this book, which draws together a series of reflections on how we will never be able to rid ourselves of such hauntings. The chapters that follow present a series of "hauntings," moving from what haunts the field of continental philosophy (chapter 1), to hauntings of our sovereign selves (chapter 2), the church (chapter 3), our words and language in general (chapter 4), and our writings by the autobiographical "I" (chapter 5). Each of these things is deeply

---

17. See, among other passages, Hosea 6:6; Isaiah 1:11–31; and Jeremiah 7:21–23.

18. I elaborate on this tension in more detail in my *Continental Philosophy and Theology*.

haunted, a reality that prevents us from every totalizing any of these representations and institutions.

Though I might wish, as so many do, to return to some fictitious, primordial point of origin that promises a form of wholeness beyond the dualities we have constructed for ourselves, I'm not sure such a thing ever really existed.

At least I'm sure that we can't find it now.

The best we can do is to be attentive and to listen to those oppressed and repressed elements within our world, even within ourselves, that cry out to be heard. Such forces have the power to upend our most cherished normative representations of ourselves, and yet this is not something to be feared. It is rather the very condition by which justice enters our world.

To live in fear of such elements, to try to cast them into utter darkness by dismissing them as antinomian, nihilistic, or heretical, is to miss the entire point of why they exist. They are there for us, calling to us to get us to see what we have ignored for far too long, those marginalized within the world around us and even those marginalized elements within *us* that we long to forget.

CHAPTER ONE

Haunting Continental Philosophy

MY DOCTORAL SUPERVISOR WAS Belgian, marked in ways both conscious and unconscious by the political tensions that have crisscrossed and colonized his politically and culturally partitioned country for centuries. Traditions are carried forward in Belgium with great respect, with an almost sacred aura, because they have often served to preserve a people in the face of its constant dissolution, whether from wars or from internal divisions. Walloons cling to their French and the Flemish cling to their Dutch so that both might maintain the legacy of their respective cultures, festivals, and idioms. Unity is precarious in such a context.

As I sat in his office one day he reminded me that a tradition should not be closed, but should, in order to be honest with itself, remain an open narrative, willing to let itself be interrupted on occasion so that it might reform itself in the face of critique or an encounter with difference. Religion, he argued, much like the German political theologian Johann Baptist Metz, is a powerful force of interruption within a person's life, welcoming disruption—at times as *revelation*, whether personal or communal—while also preserving the necessary flow of identity within its narrative.[1]

I had no reservations about the truth of what he suggested, as powerful forces of otherness and alterity permeate every existing identity. But what about a tradition that ends, I asked him? Shouldn't some traditions just simply come to a close and be finished once and for all?

That was a really good question, he replied, sitting back quietly in his chair to think. But no fuller response ever came. His job, I felt, was more inclined to preserve a tradition under scrutiny, especially as religion tries to survive in the modern critical and secular era in which we live. Christianity

1. Boeve, *God Interrupts History*. See also Metz, *Faith in History and Society*.

needed to be an open narrative in the face of secularization so that it might sustain itself, adapt, and reformulate its identity. By refusing to maintain itself as an exclusive, closed tradition or community, Christianity might provoke encounters with difference that would enable it to survive while other religious traditions died. At least, this was what one might presume to be the case.

My supervisor's work is needed and appreciated, for it allows us to see how a tradition, any tradition really, might look beyond itself in order to *be* itself. Traditions develop and evolve, despite their frequent reticence to acknowledge as much. Religious tradition, in fact, often presents itself as a sacred, immovable object that we fetishize because there is an unspoken consensus that it should be passed along forever, even as it sometimes deteriorates, crumbles, and slides into the sea. Memory all too often becomes a cult, as one author on the nature of memory has put it. "Each of us is in fact a witness to and participant of a lasting catastrophe. Our desire to shore up the past against rapid dissolution, and to keep it intact like the gold reserve, can easily become a fetish of sorts, something we can all sign up to, a zone of unspoken consensus."[2] For many, this is what religion has become in the face of those secularizing forces that seem, at this point, to be more or less ineradicable.

Perhaps, however, there are other ways to perceive the fate of Christianity in the West. This was what began to occupy my mind more immediately on that day in my supervisor's office.

Kenosis is an essential element in the Christian narrative. To empty oneself out, to pour oneself out to the point of an apparent dissolution of the self and its identity—as God did by taking the form of Jesus—is not to refuse the narrative of Christianity altogether, but it does appear to be a relinquishment of one's right to defend one's Christian identity. As some theorists and historians have recently suggested—Larry Siedentop and Gianni Vattimo among them—the secular order we currently inhabit in the West is the natural outgrowth of a Christian kenotic action that is willing to pour out its own identity in order to exhibit its truest virtue.[3] If God was willing to take on a lesser form so that a more authentic love might be brought into the world, what prevents Christians from letting go of their identities so that their faith might paradoxically flourish?

2. Stepanova, *In Memory of Memory*, 81.
3. See Siedentop, *Inventing the Individual*; and Vattimo, *After Christianity*.

This question has significant implications, but not just for the future of Christianity and the West. The kenotic impulse that brings both liberation theologies and philosophical expressions of "weak thought" to the fore is the same one that initiates a radical self-reflexive encounter with a long legacy of the myriad forms of western imperialism, from economics and politics to religion and philosophy. As daunting as the task has become in our era, every presupposition needs to be re-examined.

If it is true, for example, that continental philosophy was disseminated historically and globally through Catholic academic and missionary endeavors, as Edward Baring has suggested, then the secular era in which we now live demands a renewed investigation of just what the legacies of continental philosophy are.[4] Continental philosophy has wrestled with its limits for centuries, more recently bringing its own particular ontotheological trajectory to something of a conclusion in Nietzsche's pronouncement of the death of God.

As Calvin Warren reminds us, however, the rise of modern nihilism in the West does not merely suggest the death of God; it also signals the parameters of western colonialist and racist views.[5] Debates about secularization, atheism, and the deconstruction of Christianity directly mark the decline of ontotheology in the West, as well as a long overdue opening to non-European voices. The rise of secular forms of life becomes a critique of the West that is launched from *within* a western context, a self-reflexive gesture made in the wake of the death of Europe's God who maintained a certain political-theological legacy, while also providing liberation for those on the margins of its "civilizing," violent ethos.

The boundaries of continental thought have been further pressed through various engagements with postcolonial theory (Spivak, Bhabha), feminist philosophy (Irigaray, Kristeva, Butler) and from the perspective of race (Mbembe). Each of these critical endeavors continues to push continental philosophy to reconsider what role they can play in a contemporary global context, while also calling into question the hegemonic foundations of European thought as a whole. Pluralization, attentiveness to the limitations of western canonical forms, and an increased awareness of the realities of racial oppression all provide unique vantage points from which to sustain critiques of continental philosophy, even as its practitioners recover and rehabilitate wholly worthy elements within a vast and constantly expanding tradition.

4. Baring, *Converts to the Real.*
5. Warren, *Ontological Terror.*

What is the future of continental philosophy as it is now (somewhat) divorced from its Catholic heritage? What do the diverse global practitioners of continental philosophy today have to say about its own internal limitations? What resources active *within* European philosophy nonetheless point *beyond* European thought, causing those working in continental philosophical circles to read and engage works by non-European voices and cultures? Where do such connections lie and how might they soon become the main focal points of whatever the tradition of continental philosophy is slowly becoming? Does continental philosophy provide openings to the performance of multicultural philosophies? Why have so many global and indigenous philosophies been relegated to the margins of academia in postcolonial contexts?

Each possible answer to one of these questions is an ongoing negotiation already being addressed by those who refuse to contain philosophy within a particular hegemonic guise. And yet it is also the case that recovering philosophy as a way of life will mean nothing if it does not begin with the recognition of the limitations encountered in one's own worldview. Perhaps, in so many words, we should rename continental philosophy as North Atlantic philosophy in order to open our territorial sensibility to African, Asian, and South American philosophies, or, more specifically, Senegalese, Japanese, Confucian, or Brazilian philosophies.[6]

The questions we need to ask are more incisive still: what do we value and what do we ignore? Or, more to the point, whom do we value and whom do we ignore? Why? Do we recognize our interdependence or the complexity of the (eco)spheres we inhabit? Or do we seek only to replicate an internal, often capitalistic-imperialistic-colonialist logic of infinite expansion, profit, and possession? To seek only these latter values, as Jared Diamond highlights in his book on the demise of particular, global civilizations, is to risk cultural and societal collapse.[7]

I have benefited greatly from my reading of J. Lorand Matory's *The Fetish Revisited: Marx, Freud, and the Gods Black People Make*, in no small measure because of the way it reframes questions about what we value and why we value what we do.[8] Matory rightly denounces the modern label of the fetish, which, through its many uses in economic, psychological, and anthropological fields, assumes that the one wielding it understands a given

6. Ochieng, *Intellectual Imagination*.
7. Diamond, *Collapse*.
8. Matory, *Fetish Revisited*.

value better than someone else. As he puts it, the accuser self-righteously assumes that they know what is valuable and what is not, and they seek to impose their viewpoint upon those whom they deem "less worthy," or "less knowledgeable" than themselves. In short, those in politically, socially, religiously, and economically dominant positions get to brand those they oppress as being "fetishistic" in their beliefs concerning value, something that has historically denied black people representation in various arenas. Perhaps Matory's most revealing critical insight is that fetishism entails the "uneven assigning of agency," which inevitably leads to the complete neglect of certain persons within a given symbolic economy of representations.

I was particularly glad to hear Matory describe how he is hesitant to even use the word fetish because it tends to be pejorative and uneven in its assigned value—a colonialist remnant needing to be further interrogated. In my own work on the illusory historical boundary between fetishes and sacramental-objects (which I wrote about in *The Fetish of Theology: The Challenge of the Fetish-Object to Modernity*[9])—both being sacred objects imbued with a value far beyond their material worth—it is clear that western Christian colonialist attitudes perceived the one object to be of inestimable value while the other was deemed to be "idolatrous" and "pagan." Like the word "heresy," the connotations of such words fluctuate with time, depending on who is deemed to have the authority to affix such labels.[10] The distinction between the sacrament and the fetish ultimately served imperialistic hegemonic interests, though the distinction has stuck around to such a degree that even Christian theologians, to this day, fail to make any comparison or contrast between sacramental-objects and the material sacred objects of other traditions, most typically considering them essentially as idolatrous (such as notably with ongoing Protestant critiques of Catholic material, sacred objects).

My own evaluation was directly geared toward exposing the "fetishistic" within the "sacramental" and the "sacramental" within the "fetishistic" in order to erode the boundary between the terms and implicate everyone in the negative and positive connotations associated with both sides. I wanted not only to destabilize the hegemony of western, Christian sacraments through recourse to fetishes, but my sense was further that, as Matory puts it, we are all fetishists in some way, and, as Adorno once added, to claim that you are free of a fetishistic logic was merely to reinscribe oneself within its worst excesses at a deeper level. Again, as Matory so eloquently described

9. Dickinson, *Fetish of Theology*.

10. See, among others, Moore, *War on Heresy*.

the situation we all find ourselves in: we are all hypocritical in our assigning of values to certain things and in downplaying the value in other things.

The failure to understand the political valences and uses of fetishism results, as Matory aptly describes it, in various private, mimetic subcultures that parody oppressive hierarchical social, political, and economic relations in order perhaps simply to relieve anxiety or to create situations of carnival that, in turn, actually support a dominant status quo. BDSM, as the example he takes up in his conclusions, is not a public, political stance that enacts moments of parody in order to destabilize a given normative order—as one might argue that drag performances work to subvert gendered norms. BDSM is rather a private fantasy of reversal that allows one to return to, and so perpetuate, the governing order.

The daily hegemonic, racist relations that structure our world are not affected in the least by BDSM practice; they do nothing politically, socially, or publicly in order to change the injustices that actually permeate our world, while also perpetuating stereotypes regarding hypersexualized black bodies in order to cover up the socially symbolic "vanilla" quality of white bodies. It is in such contexts that we can see how BDSM is fetishistic in the sense of providing a false attribution of values to things that do not actually have such value. But it is also bound up with the blindness of a colonialist perspective that denigrates ("inferior") objects and bodies. That is, the imperialistic, colonialist, racist attitudes that many moderns feel they have left behind for good have only resulted in new, subtler, more insidious forms of fetishism that have yet to be recognized and called out for what they really are.

There is much to be gained by listening, and continuing to listen, to how Matory critiques the lack of autonomy and value with regard to marginalized persons and how the very label of the fetish signals a disagreement regarding the assigning of value—something often concealed in western, capitalist societies where the value of a commodity is often inherently viewed to be globally (universally) held. But, as he also notes, it is not just the commodity that is taken to be universal. Theories themselves, such as those offered by Marx and Freud regarding fetishism, are capable of becoming fetishes in order to avoid those theorists themselves being aligned with those who were marginalized and fetishized in other ways (e.g., women, black persons, etc.).

The idea that even a theory of fetishism can become a fetish—an idea described in detail in Hartmut Böhme's *Fetishism and Culture*[11]—is something that academics, especially white, male, western academics need to hear over and over and over again. The abstracted theoretical worlds

11. Böhme, *Fetishism and Culture*.

deployed in order to subjugate entire peoples and nations needs to be repeatedly unmasked. So too does the necessary work of destabilizing theoretical worlds—such as Matory does with regard to Marx's failure to account for actual black slaves in his account of the "wage slave" of white, European origin—become one that must continue to be heard over the "standard" hegemonic and subtly (and not so subtly) racist discourses that continue to dominate many academic, theoretical scenes.

I recall leaving my supervisor's office that ordinary weekday many years ago and stepping immediately into the bowels of the theology library in Leuven, Belgium—the Maurits Sabbe Bibliotheken—where accumulated centuries had brought multiple layers to the compulsion to store and catalog written knowledge. In this space I routinely felt my own desires for an ever-expanding, almost infinite library propel my inclinations toward buying books. My intuition that every field, every system of thought, every philosophy searching for its own internal consistency, should relentlessly probe its inner limits led me to believe that an opening toward otherness might appear in the cracks in the façade and might yield those transcendent insights that most truly prop up our humanity.

For years I had been slowly purchasing volumes of most major European philosophers, hoping by some unconscious fevered dream to eventually collect every work worthy of being housed under the generic banner of "continental philosophy." It was a desire for completion as much as one for mastery, and it was a longing that seemed to reside not only within me, but within most of my peers as well. To be conversant in a given academic field, I so often discovered, meant immersing oneself in its literature, placing obscure references casually dropped in conversation and lamenting professional knowledge that had not yet been personally acquired. I was drawn as much to the library and the bookstore as I was to the classroom or the colloquium because it was in those depositories and archives that my appetite for learning was more readily piqued. It was in such places that I could obtain, through asserting, my mastery.

The questions that I was then only learning to ask were not yet guideposts in my education: why do I prefer these authors to those? Why pursue this degree instead of that one? What presumptions guide this field and what new learning might destabilize them? What presupposition was I willing to risk and what one was I unwilling to let go of?

These questions, though unknown to me at the time, were of apiece with another set of questions, ones perhaps more important: how is my view of myself intertwined with the subjects I study? What happens when the narrative of self I have sought hard to construct is interrupted? What do I do when my identity is troubled by an otherness signaling limitations to the entire modern project of collecting, classifying, and organizing these knowledges? And, perhaps most directly to the point, how to renounce this desire for mastery and the many violences that it contains?

I recently reread Walter Benjamin's account of unpacking his library, and the almost utopian exhilaration of his reencounter with his own book collection. What struck me this time around was how forthright he was about the western, somewhat capitalist, somewhat imperialist ethos of it all, as reflected in the way in which ownership and possession are what guarantee one's intimacy with things.[12] This presumption is what allows him to suggest, much like those who possess great wealth, that "actually, inheritance is the soundest way of acquiring a collection."[13] To collect books as a personal library is a privileged form of scholarship, no matter whether one's personal archives are as alive as Benjamin's were or not. Though he sought to nuance his relationship to his library, which he held to be a repository reflecting the passion of the collector and not the sterile institutions that archives routinely become, there is nonetheless a collector's drive that remains potentially unexamined in relation to questions of ownership and possession.[14]

It is for this reason that I juxtapose his library with Maria Stepanova's archive of photos and letters that comprise her family's relations down through the past century or more, the very things she catalogs and interrogates in her journey through the meaning of personal history in her book *In Memory of Memory*. She types and retypes old letters, for example, until she feels that she owns them, had "internalized the logic of ownership" itself.[15] But she also recognizes the limits of such a logic in that she is able to see too closely into lives that, she believes, she has no right to investigate. The limits of historical representation, and certainly of biography too, are probed and pushed back against: "Blessed are those who destroy all the letters and diaries they don't want others to see. The written text creates a false impression of its own immortality."[16] The dead, for example, typically have their rights abused through our ability to mine their private artifacts, as they

12. Benjamin, "Unpacking My Library," 492.
13. Benjamin, "Unpacking My Library," 491.
14. Benjamin, *Walter Benjamin's Archives*, 2.
15. Stepanova, *In Memory of Memory*, 318.
16. Stepanova, *In Memory of Memory*, 320.

are "endlessly vulnerable" and humiliated through our taking possession of what they once claimed as their own.

It is by being attentive to such dynamics that Stepanova's wonder at the lives she encounters in her familial archive is displaced by a growing sense of injustice that, she feels, must be rectified.

> I believe this must change, and change within our lifetimes, just as it has changed over the last hundred years for other groups of the abused and humiliated. What unites all the minorities, puts them in the same boat (or on the same many-decked liner) is other people's sense that their subjectivity is incomplete: women who *need to be looked after*; children *who don't know what's best for them*; black people who are *like children*; the working classes who don't know *what's in their own interests*; the dead, for whom *nothing matters any more.*[17]

She faces the difficult conclusion that leaving the past behind, in essence forgetting the past, may be the only option available to us that also allows justice to be done, that retains the subjectivity of each person whose life remains their own possession. A new relationship to the past and to those long since departed is made possible through letting go of whatever truths we want to possess about them, from them. "Sometimes," she claims, "it seems like it is only possible to love the past if you know it is definitely never going to return."[18]

To unlearn past histories does not mean, however, that one is set to discover something else that is "new," for that is precisely what imperialist-colonialist desires do.[19] The "newness of the new" feeds off of colonialist and capitalist drives, causing whatever collections we maintain to constantly expand in their efforts to incorporate and appropriate whatever living reality is brought into the sterile confines of archival suspended animation.[20] Museums, as much as zoos, conscript life abundant in order to preserve what humanity otherwise will, one way or another, destroy. We welcome the pleasures of this little death so that we might survive beyond our own deaths or the other deaths that constantly surround us. Fundamentally, we wish not to hamper our inclination to preserve life in this way. "The reduction of art making to

---

17. Stepanova, *In Memory of Memory*, 319.

18. Stepanova, *In Memory of Memory*, 427.

19. Azoulay, *Potential History*, 17.

20. Azoulay, *Potential History*, 18.

the pursuit of the new drains communities of their worldliness," just as it drains us of our own world.[21]

These are the assertions of Ariella Aïsha Azoulay, for whom the task of unlearning imperial techniques for mastery means rejecting "imperial taxonomies."[22] It means undoing the museum's drive to tear objects from their living worlds in order to arrest them in time, a tactic that reverberates from the camera's shutter as much as from any museum hall. "Unlearning imperialism means unlearning what one's ancestors inherited from their ancestors, and them from theirs, as solid facts and recognizable signposts, in order to attend to their origins and render imperial plunder impossible once again."[23] It also means, she argues, turning to other shelves in the library, ones beyond our preferred authors. Having a canonical repository that identifies one's scope and horizon makes one a citizen of a particular world, one that depends on the inscription of what was once living into this particular archive. "Citizen's privileges depend on the near worldlessness of others."[24] The never-ending expansion of the museum—what Giorgio Agamben has called the *museification* of our world—means that everything is potentially subsumed by the desire to bring it within an already existing collection, to label it with an identity easily recognizable to whatever cataloging system we maintain.[25] As she continues the thought, "When imperial actors granted themselves citizenship, they continued to protect their privileges and inscribe their accumulation in different objects, institutions, and practices, thus multiplying the number of groups governed differentially."[26]

What Azoulay terms "potential history" is a way of disengaging from "imperialism's conceptual apparatus altogether," unlearning its violence brought about through unwelcomed inscription into its systematic overview.[27] Instead, she avers, we must learn to care for a common world instead of archiving the objects that exist within a given world. We must undertake the "labor of forgiveness" in order to make the world inhabitable again, thus making "reversal, restitution, or reparations . . . an inseparable part of a political ontology no less than violence is."[28] The impossible possibility of forgiveness turns on the imaginative potential lodged within history, the

21. Azoulay, *Potential History*, 61.
22. Azoulay, *Potential History*, 15.
23. Azoulay, *Potential History*, 13.
24. Azoulay, *Potential History*, 30.
25. Agamben, *Profanations*, 83.
26. Azoulay, *Potential History*, 35.
27. Azoulay, *Potential History*, 43.
28. Azoulay, *Potential History*, 57.

sense that things could have been otherwise and that they might be once again. This can only be done, she argues, by recognizing that some acts are indeed unforgivable.[29]

Azoulay imagines historians going on strike, refusing to write alternative histories until the errors of the past have been corrected, until indigenous lands and knowledges are restored, until present forms of resistance among destitute peoples are acknowledged, until the formerly colonized are allowed to undermine history, until university libraries are opened up to everyone.[30]

I wonder what it would mean for me to go on strike as a sort of divine violence or judgment visited upon the sins of the systems with which I am complicit.[31] I wonder too whether there would be any end to the rectifications of injustice that clutter the various worlds we comprise. Azoulay's desire is an antinomian one, a longing to suspend every normative measure and institution so that we might gain a renewed perspective on those traditions and identities that we cling to as assuredly as we construct them.

Likewise, some years ago, when I was conducting my aforementioned study on fetishism in the modern period—a subject truly at the heart of all desires to push against the boundaries of collecting and identifying—I came across Edward Said's reading of Freud on the latter's antinomian tendencies. Said, in a lecture given at the Freud museum in London in 2001, revealed how the opening up of an identity to that which is wholly other to it through the transgression of a normative boundary brings about a liberation of what had formerly been repressed.[32] This is the often dark terrain by which human psychology locates an experience of freedom apart from the traditions and identities that otherwise seek to, and *do*, define us.

For every assertion of a normative or universalizing claim, there are those forces that arise to undo the former's hold. Benjamin called them "weak messianic forces," which stood up to the tyrannies of a given historical representation—what Nietzsche, for his part, had called "monumental history."[33] For every account of history, there are an almost infinite number of histories that remain obscured in our view, but which, nonetheless, possess

29. Azoulay, *Potential History*, 571–72.

30. Azoulay, *Potential History*, 375–79.

31. Benjamin, "Critique of Violence."

32. Said, *Freud and the Non-European*.

33. Benjamin, "On the Concept of History," 390; and Nietzsche, *Untimely Meditations*, 68–75.

the power to upend a normative representation of "how things really were." Said was, of course, critical of any claims toward an abstract universalism.[34] The logic of colonialist history is in fact often perceived as one of abstraction to the highest degree, until something like an "absolute knowledge" is achieved but which is ultimately a distortion of lived, oppressive realities.[35] Experiences of forgiveness or grace within our representational networks are dependent upon our ability to relinquish a definitive version of events and to acknowledge the uncertainty and impossibility latent within every account of truth we might seek to give.

Voices more moderate than Azoulay are called for, ones that recognize the irreconcilable, unfading tensions between history and the minor histories that contest it, just as with theology and the plural theological forces that upend any monolithic or imperialist identity, though they are ones that must also recognize how all of us negotiate our identities in the midst of such tensions.[36]

This is not to suggest, however, that the forms of resistance Azoulay contemplates or that the antinomian impulse to strike are not valid strategies developed in response to the situations that many find themselves in. For it is not only a colonization of lands and peoples that concerns us, but also the colonization of one's psychic space, as Kelly Oliver has described it, that we are confronted with.

For Oliver, there is an endless interrogation that forgiveness enacts as an opening toward otherness—that is, a willingness to move beyond one's identity and toward that which undoes it. In this sense, being able to "transgress or revolt" against a normative order "presupposes forgiveness" as its backdrop. In her words, "Forgiveness, then, is not about forgiving the perpetrator of some crime but about forgiving the transgression that is singularity and individuality."[37] This reframing of forgiveness beyond its historical-theological signature and beyond the contexts of political pardon means that we are forced to ask serious questions about what room is or is not given in society to those who are marginalized and who transgress the normative order through their very existence. Forgiveness, she rightly contends, is about restoring subjectivity to the victim and thereby moving beyond the dictates of sovereign power that otherwise routinely envelop us.

34. Said, *Power, Politics, and Culture*, 390.

35. Guha, *History at the Limits*, 2–3.

36. Chakrabarty, *Provincializing Europe*; and Taylor, *Theological and the Political*.

37. Oliver, *Colonization of Psychic Space*, 191.

Franz Fanon, she notes, had spoken of a need for the colonized to enter a state of forgiveness, of grace in fact, where they locate their worth. "But, in a racist or sexist society," she adds, "if part of one's singular individuality is to be a man of color or a woman, this becomes a 'trespass' that is not forgiven."[38] Transgressiveness, like the force of antinomianism, is liberatory in the sense that it rebels against the law in order to reformulate the law, transforming "shame into agency."[39] Subjectivity, in fact, "requires revolt and transgression to become a singular individual, but it also presupposes forgiveness to belong to the social."[40] Denying an individual or a people their rights of revolt and forgiveness is how domination proceeds to colonize one's psychic space, and it is a step toward decolonizing the mind and exercising one's capacity for critical thought that takes place through those revolutionary and antinomian gestures that complicate our everyday political operations.[41] It is what Agamben has defined as inoperativity, and what characterizes for some his own, Benjamin-infused philosophy as a type of "pure antinomianism."[42]

It is important to note how, for Oliver, such acts of forgiveness take us beyond the economies of property and ownership that have been used for centuries to justify "colonization, exploitation, slavery, and domination."[43] Formulating an "ethics of responsibility without sovereignty," where we never cease to issue a critical inquiry about ourselves, becomes the operating norm of thought itself.[44] The space for critical thinking, for imagination and for ideas, is the radical, revolutionary space that we must never shy away from defending. It is only by occupying such a space that we are able to become responsible for our unconscious "motives, desires, and fears" that otherwise might obstruct right action.[45] "When the trespass or revolt necessary to assert singularity and authorize individuality is forgiven, then the result is not alienation but a sense of belonging and an affirmation of agency, which are as essential to psychic life as they are part of the precarious and continuous process of becoming subjectivity."[46]

38. Oliver, *Colonization of Psychic Space*, 195.

39. Oliver, *Colonization of Psychic Space*, 196.

40. Oliver, *Colonization of Psychic Space*, 196.

41. Oliver, *Colonization of Psychic Space*, 197.

42. This claim is made in Zartaloudis, *Giorgio Agamben*.

43. Oliver, *Colonization of Psychic Space*, 198.

44. Oliver, *Colonization of Psychic Space*, 199.

45. Oliver, *Colonization of Psychic Space*, 200.

46. Oliver, *Colonization of Psychic Space*, 198.

I am reminded at this point of how Theodor Adorno's response to radical student protests in the late 1960s was to advocate for more critical thought, not to leap too quickly to action when such action might be a misjudged or misguided undertaking.[47] His suggestion is shared with other contemporary philosophers who, though not shying away from direct political involvement or taking stances on controversial social issues, advocate for critical thought as the major task facing humanity that needs to be taken up resolutely again and again. We might count figures such as Slavoj Žižek and Giorgio Agamben among their number.

It is tragic, however, that Adorno's response fell somewhat upon deaf ears at the time. Indeed, his confrontation with student protesters and the radical positions they held was, many felt, the cause of his untimely death shortly thereafter. Perhaps the real issue between Adorno and his students, however, was not simply that he valued the space for critical thought while they sought action, justice, and reform. Perhaps the real issue was that, as Achille Mbembe describes it in the context of colonialism, the "master . . . practically never lets himself be *touched* by the speech of his subjects."[48] Though I will refrain from suggesting that Adorno did not listen to his students or that his students felt they were not being heard, it seems like an impasse along these lines was broached in some form.

The language of the Other is not one that the master wishes to speak— a point that too many professors and experts internalize and exhibit without much self-reflection. To refuse to speak the other's language, however, is a matter of denying hospitality to the other, as Derrida has put it on occasion. Caught in the tension between the impossibility of accepting the Other as "one of us" while also desiring endlessly that they become "like us," a good many of us, especially in the West, refuse to acknowledge the desires of the Other who asks us to recognize and hear their voice.[49]

Though it may sound extreme to suggest that the suppression of the voice of the Other is tantamount to genocide, there is a structural affinity here that we must recognize. As Mbembe describes the connection, ". . . in its structure as well as in its ornament—above all when it rested on racist and supremacist presuppositions—the colonial process always revolved around a genocidal drive. In many cases, this drive never materialized. But it was always there, in a latent state."[50] To be the Other to an established

---

47. Adorno, "Resignation," 289–93.
48. Mbembe, *Necropolitics*, 153.
49. Mbembe, *Necropolitics*, 138.
50. Mbembe, *Necropolitics*, 128.

order, community, or system is to remain in an unstable position.[51] It is one's inherent instability too that renders an individual more likely to be subjected to those acts of scapegoating needed to shore up a governing order—as the work of René Girard deftly illustrates.[52] Racism, from this point of view, functions as the placing of one's shame onto the Other, onto a scapegoat who struggles to free itself from the grip that a particular society, and its accompanying systemic oppressions, places upon an entire people.[53]

The compulsions to classify, categorize, and label that accompany modern colonial, imperialist endeavors are not separate from its treatment of black people, Mbembe continues.[54] Sharing with Azoulay's remarks a moment ago, he finds that, in opposition to such tactics, humanity must follow the slave who haunts the museums of the West and who founds the "anti-museum" as a place of refuge and of "radical hospitality."[55] The same questions that appeared earlier in the context of Azoulay's call for academics to strike appear here as well: to what degree can scholars continue to draw from continental, colonial legacies? Or, as Mbembe phrases it, "does saying it has ceased to be the world's center of gravity mean that the European archive is exhausted?"[56]

His conclusion is that European archives are not exhausted, and so not to be discarded once and for all, as new assemblages are still possible from among their ruins. Indeed, how could this not be the case when there are those among us standing at its center acknowledging fully that "in our own history the most interesting part is what we don't know."[57] Moreover, within such an archive, what white westerners in particular do not know is also what we do not know about ourselves. Such lacuna are, in fact, constitutive of us as a group—a point that James Baldwin underscored some time ago when he suggested that ". . . whatever white people do not know about Negroes reveals, precisely and inexorably, what they do not know about themselves."[58]

Though westerners working in fields heavily marked by European legacies would like to think that we have jettisoned the imperialist and colonialist pretensions that characterized our past, we no doubt carry them

51. Mbembe, *Necropolitics*, 132.
52. See Girard, *Violence and the Sacred*.
53. Mbembe, *Necropolitics*, 131.
54. Mbembe, *Necropolitics*, 158.
55. Mbembe, *Necropolitics*, 172.
56. Mbembe, *Necropolitics*, 188.
57. Stepanova, *In Memory of Memory*, 308.
58. Baldwin, "Fire Next Time," 312.

with us still. As we dig through our archives wondering where all of this is headed and whether or not our scholarship will culminate in one final, lasting vision of truth, we masquerade as Benjamin's image of the dwarf within the puppet once again, offering a theological vision that knows it must stay out of sight, though retaining its strength all the same.

In a religious world, one that was once significantly indebted to particular visions of divine history, salvation and conservation are joined together, as the divine recalls and remembers everything. Nothing is lost in such a world, and everything is retained, subject to divine judgment without end or exception. As Maria Stepanova reminds us, however, things have changed in the modern period, where "secular society takes the idea of salvation out of the equation, and in one stroke the whole construction loses its balance. Without a belief in salvation, 'conservation' becomes no more than an institutional archive: a museum, a library, a warehouse, allowing a sort of conditional and limited immortality—a greatly extended single day, the only version of *eternal life* that is possible in the emancipated new world."[59] There is perhaps a hollow feeling that remains when we view our wholly immanent life from this perspective, as we try to retain every memory, but we fail to do so, and our pale imitation of eternity falls into ruin at some point. Items, like our family photo albums, become an attempt to avert the catastrophe of death, though "the oath of fidelity to family history becomes its destruction, a parody of the resurrection of the dead: another is replaced by oneself, the known world squeezed out by the invented world, *hell is other people* becomes the family album where everyone is in their rightful place, pretending to be alive."[60]

Jean Baudrillard once imagined that history, from a European perspective, had capitulated to the fevered dreams of a hyperrealistic capitalism that only brought about the dissolution of the West. He felt that we now have to face the "radical illusion" of history that leaves European history not ended, but exposed. "We are, then, unable to dream of a past or future state of things. Things are in a state which is literally definitive—neither finished, nor infinite, nor definite, but de-finitive that is, deprived of its end. Now, the feeling which goes with a definitive state, even a paradisiac one—is melancholic. Whereas, with mourning, things come to an end and therefore enjoy possibility of returning, with melancholia we are not even left with the presentiment of an end or of a return, but only with *ressentiment* at their disappearance. The crepuscular profile of the *fin de siècle* is more or less of

59. Stepanova, *In Memory of Memory*, 86.
60. Stepanova, *In Memory of Memory*, 177.

this order, combining the features of a linear order of progress and a regression, itself also linear, of ends and values."[61]

Our attempts to produce monuments to history are doomed to eventual failure. They will fall, as they all do, and our cultural memory will consequently fade at some point over time.[62] Perhaps, as some have suggested, in order for true forgiveness to become reality, we will even have to forget those events of history—those traumatic and tragic, but also those wonderful and celebrated—that we vow in the present moment never to forget.[63] Humanity stands permanently only as it finds itself continuously situated within a vast series of ruins, the logical outcome of all of our inherently violent representations that are doomed to be surpassed and overcome as the natural course of things.[64] In Susan Stewart's eyes, we are only able to overcome the problems that plague us when we face the ruins that stand before us: "The representation and repetition of fragmentation alleviates the problem of vanished cause and sets aside certain problems of agency and finality of form."[65]

The potential of history is continuously replayed on the field of ruins, from which we select some and ignore others in order to recreate the present moment in which we reside. "For Gibbon, ruins call for remembering; for Leigh Fermor, they call for forgetting. Between attention and neglect, waking and dreaming, they cast their shadows on our thought and making."[66] We are ceaselessly engaged in acts of self-creation from among the ruins, and cultures, as much as individuals, live and die accordingly. With this thought, we are returned to the ends of traditions that now stand in ruins before us—one thinks of the cult of Mithras in ancient Rome or the Greek pantheon atop Mt. Olympus—but also the "newer" traditions cobbled together from among the ruins of what came before them. Christian theologians, starting with Augustine, used to consider it fitting that theology should take from pagan (Greek) philosophy whatever was precious and valuable—the spolia or "spoils"—just as the Israelites had once claimed the riches of Egypt before absconding to the promised land. Likewise, Christian architects made use of ancient ruins in order to shore up their staggeringly

61. Baudrillard, *Illusion of the End*, 120.

62. Stewart, *Ruins Lesson*, 269.

63. Rieff, *In Praise of Forgetting*.

64. Stewart, *Ruins Lesson*, 259.

65. Stewart, *Ruins Lesson*, 259.

66. Stewart, *Ruins Lesson*, 20.

impressive cathedrals.[67] We can note too antinomian theorists and political insurrectionists utilizing European thought precisely to overthrow the historical legacies of European hegemony.

If it is true, as Stewart claims, that ruins "arise at the boundaries of cultures and civilizations," I wonder which fields of study and which traditions will soon face their demise, and which are more equipped to survive. I wonder, too, which fields, and the traditions they sustain, best demonstrate an awareness of the nature of being ruined, as we all must be ruined someday.[68] To face one's failures, to embrace failure itself as the only way to go forward, is paramount, even essential to the task of being human at all. It is embedded in us and it is what brings about the experience of freedom that characterizes our humanity.

It is with such reflections in mind that I do not fear the fact that continental philosophy, as it has been known, is dying and the supremacy of Christianity along with it. These realities are precisely what must be embraced, not shied away from. As James Baldwin once framed matters, "One can give nothing whatever without giving oneself—that is to say, risking oneself. If one cannot risk oneself, then one is simply incapable of giving."[69] I hope I am willing to risk these traditions because I want to know what it means to understand, but, better, to give. This is why I would claim that every so-called Christian must embrace Baldwin's continuation of the thought: "It is not too much to say that whoever wishes to become a truly moral human being (and let us not ask whether or not this is possible; I think we must *believe* that it is possible) must first divorce himself from all the prohibitions, crimes, and hypocrisies of the Christian church. If the concept of God has any validity or any use, it can only be to make us larger, freer, and more loving. If God cannot do this, then it is time we got rid of Him."[70]

I often wonder how the declaration of Christianity's moral bankruptcy—a historical charge made by Baldwin that I have no desire to refute (even if it can be refuted)—abuts with the kenotic nature of Christianity.[71] How can you declare something to be morally bankrupt as an institution when the essence of the institution itself potentially refuses its own form? Wouldn't a truly kenotic Christianity be willing to pour out its own ecclesial and political identity in order that a higher truth or a more virtuous living be attained? What if Christianity relinquishes its sovereign gestures entirely,

67. Stewart, *Ruins Lesson*, 61–66.

68. Stewart, *Ruins Lesson*, xiv.

69. Baldwin, "Fire Next Time," 336.

70. Baldwin, "Fire Next Time," 314.

71. Baldwin, "Fire Next Time," 316.

to the point of no longer existing as the most faithful witness to its own internal dynamics?

There is a dissolution as disruption or state of emergency that is brought about by the "madness" of capitalism that we in the West live under, as Bernard Stiegler has described it.[72] And so, in a time when capitalism and its accompanying forces of detraditionalization ceaselessly pull a fair number of us up by our roots, we are often right to be nostalgic for a coherent and culturally rich past. It is our duty to the future to locate from among the ruins of the past a selective way forward, as Grafton Tanner has noted.[73] The secular era in which we live thereby becomes one wherein we learn to make use of the best of religious traditions, albeit in forms completely different from those these once monolithic traditions understood themselves to be. This is the cost of living in a pluralistic world that no longer feigns subservience to a single, governing master narrative. Likewise, the philosophy still yet to come will hopefully make just use of the ruins of European philosophy even as it fabricates something entirely new.

It is imperative that today we learn to develop a healthy curiosity when faced with a pluralistic world, not shying away from diversity and difference, even when performing comparative studies, especially in the domain of the everyday, becomes disorienting.[74] It is somewhat ironic then that, as Tim Connolly describes things, "the biggest impetus to fragmentation, violence, and anarchy today does not emerge from political engagement with the paradox of difference. It emerges from doctrines and movements that suppress it. Specifically, it arises from totalistic identities engaged in implacable struggles against those differences that threaten their hegemony or exclusivity. Such culture wars do not reflect too much diversity, difference, or variety; they express contending demands to control the exclusive form the nation, state, or community must assume."[75] The pushback against difference on the part of entrenched communal defenses, then, is what creates many of the problems we are facing today in terms of cultural clashes and culture wars.

Connolly contends that we should avoid the simplistic dualism of individual versus community that has often led to theoretical stalemates in the modern era. Instead, we have to recognize the complexities of communal

---

72. Stiegler, *Age of Disruption*.

73. Tanner, *Hours Have Lost Their Clocks*, 230–32.

74. Connolly, *Doing Philosophy Comparatively*, 212.

75. Connolly, *Ethos of Pluralization*, xxi.

identities that crisscross every life in our globalized world. We should not seek to reduce the impact of pluralism, but rather must continue to embrace the pluralized tensions that proliferate and claim us in varied ways. Pluralism must be further pluralized, as he puts it.

This gesture of pluralizing plurality performs a crucial negative redoubling that avoids positing a prescriptive or normative identity. It shares, then, with those calls to "secularize secularity," "alienate alienation" or "objectify objectivity."[76] Each plays out a fundamental "negation of negation" or "division of division" that resists establishing a totalitarian order because they bring about a universal position through a negative gesture rather than through the establishment of a positive, shared characteristic that always turns out to be reductive of an undefinable singularity in the end—what Foucault, Agamben, and Nancy have all referred to as forms of life lived beyond their inscription into the law.

I would argue that Connolly shares in his project with Kwame Anthony Appiah's cosmopolitan ethics, an ethics, that is, wherein one does not seek to reduce the myriad lines of influence that their world places upon them, even as such forces erode traditional communal identities. We should not converge on a single mode of life, as in the past, he finds, especially as a single communal identity is not a practical possibility for many today. Being open to difference, contradiction, and complexity in our lives is not a pathway toward nihilism and relativism, but a practical outworking of those tensions that traverse our very bodies.[77] We might think here of something like Homi Bhabha's hybrid identities, or the anti-systematic, hybrid counter-energies as Edward Said called them, as other ways to name this way of being in the world.[78] We can easily imagine, from this vantage point, a project located upon the "abyssal ruins" of tradition and identity that, in turn, gives rise to "decolonized cosmopolitan futures" alongside new creolized identities.[79]

What we engage in when facing such dynamics, I would add, is the reality of constantly conducting those impossible but necessary acts of translation, as Paul Ricoeur once put it. These acts arise from the irresolvable antinomy that we are always only speaking one language while, at the same time, never only speaking one language, as Derrida had once also observed.[80]

76. These calls can be found in the writings of Étienne Balibar, Jürgen Moltmann, and Pierre Bourdieu, respectively.

77. See Appiah, *Cosmopolitanism*.

78. Said, *Culture and Imperialism*, 334–35. See also Bhabha, *Location of Culture*.

79. Yountae, *Decolonial Abyss*, 139.

80. Ricoeur, *On Translation*; and Derrida, *Monolinguism of the Other*.

Seen through the lens of Todd McGowan, "Universality is the lack in every particular."[81] It is not a utopian dream of "total belonging," as many might otherwise understand it, because non-belonging will always haunt such dreams while simultaneously speaking directly to the plight of those excluded and marginalized from a normative order. Rather, universality leads to emancipation because it does not succumb to those particularities that abandon the universal altogether, such as racist ideologies.[82] It is only our "nonbelonging" then that is truly universal.[83] In his analysis, "Universal solidarity is solidarity with those who don't belong formed through the universality of nonbelonging."[84]

Universals, as such, only exist by referencing a lack, by pointing out what is missing and not by offering to instill within us a positive colonialist program that seeks to efface differences in order to impose a sense of sameness.[85] "The universal does not appear in the act of imposing itself on people but in the failure of any regime to fully impose itself."[86] Universals are thus presented to us only through an absence, just as, one might argue, the only authentic representation of something is manifested in demonstrating our failure to accurately represent it. Correcting the misperception that universality is something imposed upon us that we must reject in order to cease the oppression of the marginalized, McGowan provides another avenue from which to view this most misunderstood of principles in our contemporary struggles regarding identity politics: "The nonrealization of the universal is fundamental to universality itself. The absence of a fully realized universal is the essence of universality because it is the result of mastery's failure. The universal is just another name for the impossibility of complete belonging. Consequently, we access universality through the struggle to realize it, not through proclamations about its future reality."[87] In other words, no one truly belongs to whatever categories they have subscribed to or to whatever labels are foisted upon them. By recognizing our inability to ever fully coincide with our social, political, economic, cultural, and religious identities, we then, and only then, enter into a universal space of nonbelonging where we rightly contest each and every identification.

81. McGowan, *Universality and Identity Politics*, 45.
82. McGowan, *Universality and Identity Politics*, 50–51.
83. McGowan, *Universality and Identity Politics*, 63.
84. McGowan, *Universality and Identity Politics*, 68.
85. McGowan, *Universality and Identity Politics*, 71.
86. McGowan, *Universality and Identity Politics*, 72.
87. McGowan, *Universality and Identity Politics*, 78–79.

Nonbelonging is also, I would argue, locatable in Paul's reading of the Christian failure to achieve a permanent identity, which shares, along with McGowan, in how "Universality is not the uniform but the absence that puts subjects at odds with themselves. The struggle on behalf of the universal is always also a struggle against oneself."[88] The focus of a genuine universality is upon the reality of how no one really belongs to any identity that is given to them. Whether we call this the Pauline secondary division of all primary social-identitarian divisions as Agamben does, or whether we seek to rehabilitate a version of Adorno's negative dialectics as a non-identitarian logic, or whether we reread Hegelian dialectics as producing no "third term" but remaining caught in the antinomy of thesis and antithesis—all of which are defensible positions undertaken by many today—we are capable of grasping an apophatic methodology that produces a sense of universality in a wholly negative manner. Whichever viewpoint we take, there is arguably little difference between calls for a negative universality and the struggles of religious radicals bent on antinomianism, between black nihilists seeking the end of white mythology and its accompanying metaphysics, and queer theorists pondering the limits of antinormativity.[89]

In suggesting such a nexus of relations, I am echoing pleas for a universality "of what is not," as William Franke puts it, a universality based on apophatic methods that defies any categorization and upends whatever attempts we might make to name the unnameable. Franke's own work seeks to develop a negative universality that resonates with a distinction made by Derrida between seeing deconstructionism as a negative operation with no historical telos and the traditions of negative theology that are still too indebted to a particular religious tradition to be purely apophatic (or purely antinomian).[90] To maintain a true apophaticism, one must detach from every tradition to some degree, evidencing an irresolvable tension at the heart of every identification. In his words, "Of course, this places apophasis as an academic discipline into contradiction and conflict with the very principle of an academic discipline."[91] What we are formulating is very much a

---

88. McGowan, *Universality and Identity Politics*, 172.

89. One can sense the antinomian tendencies toward revolt against normative order in suggestions such as this one concerning Afropessimism: "After the conference, I realized that he was no different from most White academics who dabble in Afropessimism for their own ends without regard for the fact that they are holding a grenade that has no pin. Afropessimism is a looter's creed: critique without redemption or a vision of redress except 'the end of the world.' In the hands of a Marxist academic it tends to be corrupted and contorted into something with no purchase for Black revolt." Wilderson, *Afropessimism*, 174.

90. See Derrida, "Sauf le Nom."

91. Franke, *On the Universality*, 372.

methodology of the oppressed, as Chela Sandoval describes it, a means of locating a "third meaning" beyond every reductive binary logic that would foreclose upon the complexity of our shared global human existence.[92] It is through our attentiveness to this elusive "third thing" that we are able to deconstruct the academic divisions that keep theories separate and isolate particular fields within their traditional academic guise.

A negative form of universality is necessary because it is the only way by which we might experience the essence of freedom. As McGowan has already noted, "In a world of competing particulars, there is no possibility for an emancipatory breakthrough."[93] Those arguments made to the effect that there is no neutral ground between competing traditions from which to judge the value of those traditions are likewise revealed for what they are: self-referential justifications for a particular communal tradition that refuses to consider the universality of nonbelonging and so the force that closes its ears to any external tradition or otherness.[94] To every enclosure that cultivates an exclusivist perspective or sows the seeds of racism, there is the urge to promote a dis-enclosure, as Jean-Luc Nancy describes it, that opens us up to the negative spaces of identity.[95]

McGowan takes critical aim specifically at Adorno's championing of a particularist non-identitarian stance in opposition to the totalitarian gestures of universalism.[96] The misreading that takes place in Adorno's thought, he wagers, is that Nazism was not opposed to Judaism because of the latter's particularity but because of its universal appeal: every person could potentially be "contaminated" by their Jewishness.[97] Nazism, on the contrary, with its all-too-particular racist claims, *lacked* universality and this is precisely what it hated *in* Judaism.[98] Adorno's efforts to critique all attempts at universality and to align them with totalitarian dreams thereby misreads the true nature of the universal.[99]

Adorno's non-identitarian philosophy resonates with antinomianism in that it refuses to align itself with any institutional, and so potentially totalitarian, order. It is the thorn in the side of all identity that reminds us of

92. Sandoval, *Methodology of the Oppressed*, 182.

93. McGowan, *Universality and Identity Politics*, 211.

94. See, in particular, MacIntyre, *Whose Justice? Which Rationality?*

95. Mbembe, *Critique of Black Reason*, 35. See also Nancy, *Dis-enclosure*.

96. McGowan, *Universality and Identity Politics*, 91–92.

97. McGowan, *Universality and Identity Politics*, 95.

98. McGowan, *Universality and Identity Politics*, 106.

99. At the same time, however, I would argue too that there is a negative dimension active within both McGowan's characterizations of universality and Adorno's negative dialectics that perhaps places them closer to one another than McGowan admits.

how unjust our world continues to be. Yet, as McGowan rightly notes, there is yet another way to perceive the universal that we cannot let go of, for it is the only way that something like justice might be perceptible in our world.

Continental philosophy, and the Christian-Catholic ethos that has permeated it for centuries, is coming to a close in terms of its hegemonic hold upon both western thought and global plurality as a whole. Continental philosophy has failed to include everyone, and rightly not everyone can belong to its discourses. Philosophers working on continental thought in the United States, for example—and I count myself among their number—often wonder where they belong, and where their focus should be. At the very least, there are important questions to ask when considering how this tradition is facing its end, though perhaps none more important than this one: when do we allow ourselves to become other *to* ourselves so that we might achieve a freedom apart from the ways that we have identified our sense of belonging, so that we might access the negative form of universality that McGowan describes?

This question has driven religious and political antinomians for centuries, condemned heretics to be burned at the stake, instigated Reformation-era impulses to tear down the structures that be, motivated contextual cries for liberation from the margins of discourse and society, and it still brings its powerful wager before us today.

Traditions come and go, just as identities and communities dissolve and reform, but the time has come to grasp more fully the necessary and necessarily kenotic dynamics that permeate every dissolution of identity so that we might lessen the violence that ceaselessly prevents us from embracing the otherness that defines us because we are too busy projecting it onto one another.

CHAPTER TWO

Haunting the Sovereign Self

IN THE HISTORY OF political theology there are some truths that consistently appear and reappear, and which serve to underscore how theology often legitimates a particular political configuration, such as how one reigns sovereign over both themselves and others alike. Rather than embrace relational models of interdependency, which generally involve some recognition of plurality and difference, western theology has more often engaged in blatant attempts to justify through metaphysics an almost wholly autonomous existence. God is typically depicted as wholly beyond the machinations of humanity, and humankind, for its part, seeks to legitimate rulers who are almost entirely detached from any form of accountability. From Pope Boniface VIII's fourteenth century papal bull claiming authority over all matters both spiritual and temporal, to the legitimation of modern-day nation-states, autonomy becomes the force that guarantees one's sovereignty in a theo-political context.

If the United States was subject to the laws of another country, for example, it would limit its ability to govern itself, hence any claim it might make to be sovereign. This is why certain political voices within this country frequently dislike things like the United Nations, a treaty against using land-mines, the International Criminal Court or a Supreme Court Justice who cites another nation's laws in their rulings, as each of these things appears to curb its sovereign power—what is considered the right to self-rule. It is no surprise to me that a nation founded through revolution, with a sense of its own sovereign claims, is capable of breeding so many libertarians who demand the right to self-rule and to enforce that right through an accompanying right to "bear arms."[1]

1. Immediately after typing the above sentence, I received an email from the Illinois

To be sovereign means to be in control of oneself and one's own destiny. It enables one to assert a type of self-governance that cannot be superseded by another's rule, and so it inadvertently cuts off those relationships that might actually prove helpful in seeing the faults within one's own methods—those models of interdependency that seemingly "weaken" us through the recognition of our responsibility for others. This is one of the reasons, among others, that I will refer to this type of autonomous self as "masculine," as stopping to ask for directions for many men is already a concession that one does not know what they are doing, but must rely upon others to establish a sense of orientation within a given space and time.

Men, from a very young age in this stereotypical generalization I am making, are taught to be autonomous beings—islands, as it were—who are only capable of being lords of their own castles insofar as they can demonstrate their propensity to act unilaterally to accomplish the extreme actions of their will. Men, like the sovereigns that they seek to become, make decisions and take action before thinking through the consequences because that's what "real men" do. They perpetuate, and exaggerate, the illusions of sovereign power because they are instructed to do so by the communities that shape them.

To abstract oneself to the point of denying one's own material embodiment, as men are also often wont to do, is precisely what I have elsewhere called the "fetish of theology"—a blatant attempt to remove oneself from the material conditions of existence in order to assert sovereign force over those others who do appear to be materially dependent—how indigenous fetishists and women alike are often framed culturally, politically, and religiously.[2] Christian missionaries had once tried to label West African sacred objects as fetishes while refusing to concede that their own religious material items (e.g., sacramental objects, crucifixes, relics of the saints, and so on) were also selected moments of transcendence within an immanent materiality. Civilization, in fact, has often meant little more than the ability to detach oneself from, and so obscure, the material conditions of one's own existence, involving anything from the reality of economic and labor conditions to the realities of one's own bodily needs.

I first arrived at this notion of theological fetishes when visiting the colonialist Africa museum in Tervuren, Belgium, where looted African holy objects were on display everywhere, in a country where no one would dare

---

Conservation Foundation alerting me to the fact that "There's still time to win five guns!" in their raffle. I'm starting to be reminded of why, from time to time, I read theologians who make a defense of both their faith and the right to own a gun so that their religious claims, even just symbolically, might be upheld. See, e.g., Raschke, *Force of God*.

2. See Dickinson, *Fetish of Theology*.

put on exhibit a consecrated Catholic sacrament, such as a eucharistic host.[3] To note this difference, one part of a specific political-theological nexus of relations, wasn't just to observe a contradiction: it was to note where the reins of power lie within this Catholic, European nation and so to also sow the seeds that might potentially undermine its authority through exposing its contradictions. To fail to notice the overlap between these African fetishes and Catholic sacramental objects is to fail to see the hegemonic relations that have structured western political theology for centuries. To live in such a state of detachment is to fail to recognize where the possibilities for liberation actually lie.

What I saw in Tervuren is the same detachment from the material conditions of one's existence that most typically places women's bodies on a very different socio-cultural-political plane of existence than male bodies. Women's bodies are theologically molded to specific coordinates, governed by those theological signatures that are destined to be inscribed upon those bodies as part of "nature," whereas men are often able to abstract from their bodies in order to reside in the sphere called "mind" or some sort of staged, "pure" rationality taken as a form of transcendence from the body.

Much of western culture on the whole has too often hidden behind racist judgments of this sort: we, westerners, can objectively observe and label the other's "primitive" materialistic superstitions while not taking part in such activity ourselves. Somehow, we (westerners, men) have escaped such material limitations through the abstract powers of reason itself—what is perhaps the greatest myth that the modern age still propagates in multiple contexts. Breaking down the boundary between the fetish and the sacrament, for example, and so allowing ourselves to critique Bible-wielding fundamentalists as really fetishists at heart, is only one way to widen our criticisms of sovereign power and the (mostly western) theologies that have buttressed their imperialistic, racist claims in the modern period.

The reality is that we all have fetishes that we hardly even comprehend the existence of. We have myriad ways of working through our embodied existence and the material dependencies that having a body entails. As Roberto Esposito has pointed out, our legal systems make distinctions between persons and things, but have no way of calculating which category the body belongs to.[4]

Fetishes are material attachments that we construct in order to help us deal with those contexts in our lives where meaning is overdetermined—that

---

3. "Fetish Modernity," Royal Museum for Central Africa, Tervuren, Belgium, April 8 to September 4, 2011.

4. Esposito, *Persons and Things*.

is, where too many symbols and representations clash in ways we can't mentally suture together. Fetishes are a material embodiment of a redoubling of the self. Our failure to make sense of our lived, embodied reality literally results in a dependence upon a particularly fascinating scrap of material reality, and it matters little what this material reality is, with money and the exposed parts of a human body often doing the trick for most.

Our fetishes will always fail to provide a solid foundation for meaning to cohere and so we return to them again and again in the hopes that they will yet provide enough comfort to deal with the absence of a consistent narrative that we can sovereignly control. The failure of our fetishes, just like the failure of our representations of reality, teaches us a good deal about who we are, however, should we be mature enough to listen. In fact, accepting the failure of our fetishes to ever satisfy us is actually the key toward finding a liberation from their severe emotional hold over us.

In other words, Paul's distinction made in his letters in the Christian scriptures between the flesh and the spirit has yet another application for us: embracing our failure to ever fully be identified with our externally manifested, embodied state is precisely what we need to do, though we can't be completely abstracted, or spiritualized, from our embodied lives either. We return to our communities and our identities, knowing that these things do not fully define us and that we only utilize them in order to be understood by one another. To think that they could do more for us—that we could fully identify with them without remainder—is precisely the fascist fetish par excellence. It's no wonder that a good many men who are exceedingly willing to overidentify with their claims to power also have some sort of closeted fetish. We should never be surprised when this occurrence is suddenly revealed as it so often routinely is.

When the fetishes of our lives fail us, we are forced to confront the actual material conditions of our existence and so to take a cold, hard look at the lives we are living for real. When the fetishistic aura of the attractive, sexualized other fades, we see only the vulnerable, naked body before us, shorn of its sexual allure, less than what we take sovereignty to be, but, for that reason, more likely to be embraced as a human being with human bodily needs (e.g., for warmth, food, to use the bathroom, etc.). We know this difference all-too-well, and it's why a fully naked body could be shown on prime time television when the movie is *Schindler's List*, while, in the fetish column, Janet Jackson's nipple at a Super Bowl halftime show could spark such cultural outrage.

We all have fetishes, and we can't simply do away with them. We can only, instead, point out where our fetishes fail us and where we are forced to confront the material conditions of our existence, even of our own bodies, in this space of failure. This is why we also can't do away with the desire to be sovereign, as it structures our sense of self and belonging to a particular world and a particular narrative. But what exactly is the political-theological legacy of sovereignty in the West that speaks most loudly to us today when we contemplate the narrative of the self that we all construct and govern?

The concept of sovereignty can be seen prominently on display in the most fundamental of philosophical and theological statements about human and divine existence alike. I am referring to the act of redoubling that seems to crop up in nearly every major book that deals with such subjects throughout the centuries. It is the circularity of the act of redoubling—often portrayed theologically as a story of redemption that returns one to the place of innocence from which they began as a true return to the self—that brings us face to face with the contradictions of sovereignty and yet at the same time how sovereignty is an essential part of human consciousness itself. We are only able to be human, I would claim, insofar as we engage in these acts of redoubling. It is no coincidence, then, that such acts are central to religious narratives and the metaphysical worlds bound up with them. Redoublings are therefore fictive and illusory, though they are also the condition for a shared cultural intelligibility of the self.

Take, for example, how Aristotle once defined God as the purest act of "thinking about thought" for all of eternity. This redoubling of a concept—*thinking* about *thinking* itself, which is what Hegel would define as the Absolute, or the "concept of the concept"—is what creates an abstract space apart from the immediacies of our lived reality.[5] We literally open up a space for abstract thought by thinking about the process of thinking itself. No longer are our thoughts tied to the immediate situation we find ourselves in—i.e., we think, "Oh there's an apple in that tree. I think I'll go pluck it and eat it." We are also capable of thinking about those immediate unreflective thoughts themselves. Suddenly, instead of just thinking about picking an apple and eating it, we are thinking about why we want an apple in the first place and what good that apple would do to prevent the doctor from coming round more often to inspect our health.

There is in such acts a deliberate reflexive tendency toward abstraction and transcendence, and so too the possibility of being removed from the material conditions of existence. Hence the *desire* for power becomes the always addictive *fetish* of power. Hence the man who ignores his bodily needs in order to assert his strength as a form of dominance over others.

5. Aristotle, *Metaphysics*; and Hegel, *Science of Logic*.

Hence too, as Derrida pointed out, the tendency of the author to claim to be the first to critically, insightfully make a claim that no one else has made before in order to be sovereign as author.[6] God is the ultimate example of such redoubled desires, but so is the oppressed minority or nation-state today, begging to be given its autonomy and freed of its serfdom to more powerful agents.[7]

In other words, and despite the negativity that often accrues around explorations of sovereign power today, the self-reflexive act of redoubling is what enables me to make a narrative of my life a meaningful narrative *for* me. I can take my story and examine it, shape and reshape it, present it to others and myself at the same time. To suffer an interruption of this narrative, whether self-inflicted through lying, memory loss, or self-harm, or to have it interrupted by an external, perhaps even violent, force, introduces the possibility of compromising one's sovereignty over oneself. To fail to have a self-narrative that is autonomous to some degree creates the conditions for forms of personal instability.

Philosophy begins in the act of redoubled, or self-reflexive, thought. We are able to define ourselves *as* human through this capacity to engage in self-reflexive, redoubled thinking. As should surprise no one, this is how we humans have traditionally placed ourselves atop the animal kingdom, sovereign lords over all of the other "unreflective" species that litter this small globe. Theology, with its metaphysical construction of the universe, provides a narrative to legitimate human dominance, though, to be truthful, the only thing that separates the human from every other creature is precisely an act of redoubling: the human is the animal that recognizes itself as human.[8] Should it be a further shock to us that there is a long history within western monotheism of labelling the deity supreme with redoubled titles like "lord of lords" and "god of gods," or that this deity even uses redoubled phrases to identity himself (e.g., God's name as the ultimate redoubled tautology: "I am who I am")?

To be sovereign, as the western God frequently demonstrates, means nothing more than to declare oneself *as* sovereign. In essence, I *become* sovereign because I say that I *am* sovereign. This is why the Hebrew God finds it imperative to declare himself to be the Lord and to have no other gods before him. The circle must be complete, without interruption, an entire narrative reflected back onto itself. Any person who worships such a god must learn to enter into the circle of uninterrupted divine self-reflexivity

6. Derrida, *Beast and the Sovereign.*

7. See Sarr, *Afrotopia.*

8. Agamben, *Open.*

where the human being becomes translucent so that the divine narrative alone is what is reflected clearly, directly back onto itself. To do this is at the same time, however, to worship the very foundations of our own humanity, of our consciousness and our self-proclaimed position as the most dominant creature on this planet. It is, as secular humanist critics have on occasion rightly suggested, to define religion as the worship of sovereign power itself.[9]

Metaphysics has historically been engaged in providing justification for the ultimately unjustifiable position we find ourselves in. There is no way to legitimate the worship of one god over another, the hegemony of one people over another or humanity's dominance over every other creature, just as there is no way to explain why we recall or tell certain stories about ourselves over other stories, or the advent of consciousness itself. We simply worship these things as they grant us a sense of sovereignty over ourselves, and consequently over others. Take, for example, the circular contradictions inherent in justifying God's existence. This goes back to Aristotle's "unmoved mover" as first cause of all that exists, which frequently appears to many people to be the only sound proof for God's existence.

As religious argument in the modern period typically goes: how could something so complex as the human being appear out of nowhere? There must be an intelligent deity who has designed life as we know it and who is the foundation for all the complex life that follows. This is typically the same metaphysical speculation that posits at the same time, however, that an extremely complex deity did precisely just that—appeared out of nowhere as the cause of everything else that followed.[10] This circular argument seeking to legitimate itself is precisely the best way to notice the embodied contractions of redoubling that are also its hallmark gesture.

In other words, the insoluble contradiction of redoubling that gives birth to divine existence is *the* issue that metaphysics tries to resolve, but which is really an attempt to legitimate and ground the existence of human consciousness itself. The complexity and origin of consciousness is not understandable, so we simplify and, moreover, project its insoluble redoublings onto an alleged divine being. God becomes the container, so to speak, of what Derrida called the "metaphor of metaphor" which lies at the heart of all metaphysical speculation.[11]

I will repeat the radical argument that I want to make more clearly: philosophy is what human beings utilize, not only to abstract themselves

9. See the arguments made in Zuckerman, *What It Means to Be Moral*.

10. Zuckerman, *What It Means to Be Moral*, 23.

11. Derrida, "White Mythology."

from the material conditions of lived reality, but also to proclaim themselves as the sovereign selves that we are. We rely upon this capacity for self-reflection to be who we are, and to stand tall and mighty over all the other creatures on this planet. But this activity also brings us to the specific impasse that we encountered a moment ago regarding a complex god's existence: we utilize the redoublings characteristic of sovereignty in order to establish a sense of self while also having to recognize that they are a fiction of sorts, brought into existence through the very acts of calling and recalling them into existence. We are subject, perhaps even victims, to our own propensity to assert ourselves. We reside in contradiction with ourselves and this is precisely what gives rise to our sense of ourselves in the first place.

One of the philosophers who most directly dealt with this impasse was Immanuel Kant, who spoke about how our natural capacity for reason dictated to us a series of oppositions, or antinomies, that were impossible to resolve, but which were constitutive of reason.[12] One of these is: the world has a beginning and the world has no beginning. Both appear to be true to our minds, and neither can be proved or disproved. Another is: everything seems to happen spontaneously, with no predetermined plan, though it also appears at times as if everything happens according to the natural laws that govern our world. These contradictions remind me of the articles I see every so often about how love is just a determined chemical reaction versus those who would say it is a wholly free decision. We can keep going around in circles with these arguments, and many people do just that. We hone our humanity through these circular acts of redoubling by doing so.

Philosophy, at the same time, is what allows us to escape from the immediacy of unreflective experience and the way it can impose itself upon us in an almost violent fashion. This is why philosophical thought, at its core, is always a step back from violent actions, in order not just to promote nonviolence and to cease the creation of victims—even the victims we become to ourselves—but to at least allow room for critical thought about violent action to emerge.

Religion, at its best, does much the same thing, though there are many religious mythologies, to be sure, that conceal violence rather than philosophically reveal its mechanisms, as the work of René Girard illustrates.[13] Western metaphysics, I would claim, has been party to both sides of the equation, at times legitimating violent domination, while at other times serving as a laboratory for working out the implications of redoubling for our human existence.

12. Kant, *Critique of Pure Reason*.
13. Girard, *Violence and the Sacred*.

When does a metaphysical justification for sovereignty become a legitimation for violence, however, and when does it become a critical-philosophical revelation and denunciation of violence?

The only true correlate to these positive acts of redoubling that strive to guarantee one's sovereignty, whether human or divine, is to institute another type of redoubling, but in a negative sense: the negation of negation, or what some have called the division of division. If the aim of every positive redoubling is to establish a sense of identity out and above every other thing, then the negative act of redoubling is geared more toward taking whatever identity you already have—and which is constructed upon an already existing social, political, cultural, economic, or religious division—and dividing it again.

The philosopher Giorgio Agamben has made the connection between this negative form of redoubling and its religious expression in the letters of one of the founders of Christianity, Paul.[14] For Paul, every identity is based on some prior social division, like the split between the Jew and the Gentile that defined the ancient Israelite world. What Paul noticed was that some identities believe themselves to be potentially dominant over other identities: in his context, Jew over Gentile, male over female, free citizen over slave. And yet every identity could be further subdivided so that its hold on a person was lessened, and their ability to reach out to others, even those deemed "less" than oneself, could be related to differently.

Each Jew, he reasoned, could be a Jew in the flesh or in the spirit (or ideally both, to be sure). It was possible to be a Jew in name only, but not really one at heart, just as it was possible for someone to be a Jew in spirit though not one literally, as through their mother's family tree. If a non-Jew, or Gentile, could be a Jew in spirit if not in the flesh, then what was to stop non-Jews from following this Jewish guy named Jesus who had been killed for saying too many wildly speculative theological things? Paul concluded that nothing should stop them, and eventually, after an argument that nearly destroyed the early church, Peter and the other followers of Jesus agreed.

This is what I am calling the critical-philosophical approach, one that seeks to lessen the violence of an imposed (metaphysical) identity brought about through positive acts of redoubling. It is what makes a certain portion of the Judeo-Christian heritage not just a religion, but a philosophy. This goes some way toward explaining too why certain atheist philosophers

14. Agamben, *Time that Remains.*

have argued more recently for a "return to religion," specifically this Pauline philosophical wager, in a contemporary context.[15]

Though this will initially sound like an issue of interest only to Christians, the tension between law and grace (or freedom)—or normativity and any act performed in order to avoid linguistic-cultural-political encoding—is actually a deeply philosophical conundrum that humanity still has little idea how to sort out. What Christianity attempted to do was to resolve the Judaic impasse between its legalistic and prophetic elements by appearing to take a more liberal, open stance toward Jewish Torah. Those pesky debates between Jesus and the Pharisees have very much to do with presenting what appeared to many to be a unilateral opposition to everything kosher.

If this were the case, then Jesus's position would be one of an antinomian flavor—that is, he would be taking a radical stance opposed (*anti*) to all law (*nomos*). For every defender of the Torah who cried out that God wanted his people to follow the rules, here was Jesus claiming that you don't have to follow the laws at all. Jesus appears as quite the rebel, always poised to disregard the normative order of religious, and social, well-being.

In the modern period, religiously orthodox persons often refer to such antinomian impulses as nihilistic in that they appear to disregard all custom, tradition, community, and anything that smacks of normative identifications. They would be in agreement with Martin Luther who had to temper his own early theological claims for freedom from church authority when he saw his own followers disregarding *all* law, producing a situation wherein he had to argue *for* the existence of law in his *Antinomian Theses*.[16] It almost doesn't matter if we're talking about religious worshippers playing guitars during a Catholic mass or hippies of the late 1960s appearing to upend centuries of sexual morality. It is all potentially an end-of-the-world apocalyptic scenario for those wishing to maintain the status quo. It should be no surprise that many historians have referred to events as wide ranging as the Reformation and Woodstock as both being antinomian.

A problem arises, however, when we consider the line from the Gospels where Jesus says he didn't actually arrive on the scene in order to abolish the law, but only to *fulfill* it, as in he isn't trying to be antinomian, but rather to bring the law to its intended destination. Couple this with the fact that he often appeared content to "break" the rules should the circumstances require it—the sabbath was made for humans, not humans for the sabbath,

---

15. See, among others, Agamben, *Time that Remains*; Badiou, *Saint Paul*; and Taubes, *Political Theology of Paul*.

16. Luther, *Only the Decalogue Is Eternal*.

for example—and we are facing a philosophical quandary the likes of which we are still scratching our heads about.

What exactly does it mean to *fulfill* the law and not simply do away with it, though his actions appear to be doing away with it?

In a somewhat surprising way, I would suggest that something as potentially obfuscating as Hegelian dialectics might actually provide a helpful illustration of the problem, and a potential solution. The common (mis) reading of Hegel's dialectics is that you have a position, say a normative law, that comes into contact with its opposite, as with an antinomian stance. These two polarized opposites come into contact with each other, like warring factions at a school board meeting, and you end up producing something new, a third position that we might call a synthesis. This synthesis seems to be the best of all possible things because it comes out of the previous positions but represents their union. Thesis meets antithesis produces synthesis. It is generally understood to be just this simple.

The problem with this reading of Hegel is that this isn't exactly what Hegel was up to, as many of his learned commentators have been arguing since even before his death. As some of his readers today argue, there really is no need to proceed to a synthetic "third term," but only to keep the two poles suspended in opposition to each other in some fashion.[17] The law will always contain within it an impulse to see its own undoing, as Freud had once described the death drive.[18] And every inclination to take something apart and to stand alone without any governing structure will always harbor a desire to bring order to the chaos. The confrontation of a thesis, or law, with an antithesis, or antinomian drive, does not result in a new form of perfected reality that will have borne no criticism because it is beyond fault. This was, in short, the Marxist-Communist mistake in assuming that Hegel had foretold of a stage in history wherein we could actually realize a utopian existence.

We desire solutions to what seem like intractable problems because we want a feeling of resolution and certainty that, unfortunately, and consistently, evades human existence. We want to progress forward, reaching new heights of achievement and success, and we don't want to be told that we can't conquer everything we perceive as an obstacle. Despite this reality, however, our colonialist, imperialist, capitalist, racist, sexist, and homophobic impulses don't abate altogether. In fact, we tend, as a human race, to dig ourselves in even further with the illusion that we can achieve, once

17. See, among others, Jameson, *Valences of the Dialectic*; and Žižek, *Less Than Nothing*.

18. Freud, *Beyond the Pleasure Principle*.

and for all, a stunningly beautiful, entirely consistent, eerily harmonious perfection that erases any polarized tensions within us. We abstract in order to transcend, and we do so with those positive redoublings that give rise to metaphysical speculation in the first place.

So, what word do we use to describe a state where the law is not surpassed but only fulfilled, a state which causes us to look at the law differently—not to adhere to it so closely, as if no other options existed to us, as if no critique could be mounted against it—to realize that the law can be undone quite easily? *And yet*, what word do we use to describe the state where the law must also be maintained, in some sense, if we are to be the symbolic, language-wielding animals that we are and so to actually understand one another?

Antinomian doesn't work as this term, because it is established in opposition to the law, as a protest against it, and as it perhaps needs to be. When a political impasse is reached because an issue of justice has been ignored or repressed, it makes sense that some people take up the radical position of wanting to do away with the unjust institution in the first place. The many calls to do away with police in the United States because of the racially unjust policing system are but one example.[19]

One commentator on this situation has, however, coined the term *hypernomian* to try to capture the essence of what is taking place in the attempt to go *beyond* the law while also remaining rooted *in* it.[20] I think this term contains the essence of what we are trying to access. However, the fact that we still don't have a proper word that has received anything like common recognition or usage among most people indicates that we are still trying to figure out what Jesus was suggesting. Regardless, I want to argue that he was making a major philosophical point capable of reinventing our relationship to law, institutions, communities, traditions, and any other stable marker of identity in our lives, self-narratives included.

The early Christian Paul seemed to have something like *hypernomian* in mind when he spoke of the flesh/spirit division, I would argue, because this secondary division of a more primary division between Jew and non-Jew (Gentile) effectively undid the social and religious representations that people heavily relied upon for their sense of self. In suggesting this secondary division, Paul was able to find a way *beyond* the laws that bind humans while still embodying those very same laws of identity.

Consider, for example, how he claimed to act like a Jew with the Jews and like a Gentile with the Gentiles, upholding both normative identities

19. Warren, *Ontological Terror*.
20. Wolfson, *Open Secret*.

while also undercutting the force of both, as he stood in-between worlds. To the religious fundamentalist today, he wouldn't even be a deplorable "cafeteria" Christian, picking and choosing his beliefs. He would be an apparent relativist, adopting whichever identity suited him at a given time. This would, however, be far from the truth that he was carefully adopting.

To be a Christian was, philosophically, an act of negating the externally imposed identity so as to adhere to an internal marker of the self that could not be captured by any normative representation or law. He could therefore adopt any representative identity because he was truly bound by none of them. That was the freedom he was capable of experiencing, and it was some pretty potent stuff to behold, especially during an era when slaves were considered well beneath Roman citizens, and women were considered the property of men, but in which he suggested that, in Christ, there was neither slave nor free person, neither male nor female. Here was a movement that was willing to allow both oppressed groups a seat at the table, with each and every individual being potentially equal to anyone else.

I call Paul's move a philosophical one and not just religious because it is an emancipatory logic that we are still trying to get our heads around. Though Paul may look terrible to some according to today's standards by suggesting that a runaway slave should go back to their master, as he advised Onesimus to do in his brief letter to Philemon, he was only able to suggest this tactic because he believed that none of us are held to these identities at all. I imagine he would say, if he were around today, that if we can leave behind the oppressive dualisms that would see one side dominate over another, then we should embrace whatever freedom we can get, when we can get it, because none of these identities have a real hold over us.

When Paul makes the provocative pronouncement that, in such a freedom, there is neither slave nor free person and that this division doesn't really exist because we are capable of dying to such an identity, we get the sense that Paul would be for the abolition of slavery and excited to see so many people freed of such a heavy burden. He clearly imagined that the Jew/Gentile divide could be further divided by the flesh/spirit one—the fundamental gesture that gave birth to the new form of Christianity. And, to be frank, he suggests too that the male/female boundary might also fall someday because that one too can be further subdivided. Someone might appear to be a man in the flesh, but female in spirit and we might just have to embrace that reality too, and vice versa. The fact that we are only now just beginning to see what that might look like culturally, socially, is exciting, but is also a sad sign that we have failed for far too long to grasp what is really going on here with this particular philosophical trajectory.

I'm labelling Paul's move here as a philosophical one because it resembles exactly what Hegel does when he focuses, in the same voluminous pages where he describes dialectics, on a central move he labeled the negation of negation. The negation of negation is how we take what is other to us and make it a part of us, without, however, doing away with it altogether. It is our access to universality. Essentially, we grow and transform because we negate what we once were, allowing us to become something new. But, then, after some time, we negate the new thing we have become (the original negation), what was once opposed to the past, by becoming opposed to even this initial opposition. We are thus propelled into a series of never-ending spirals away from and toward both sides, again and again, hopefully enriching us along the way as we never really lose anything we once were, only gaining new perspectives and facets on ourselves time and again.[21]

Paul was more than aware of the vulnerability that such identity dynamics bring. He was in fact acutely observant of how dividing one's identity *makes us* vulnerable, internally to ourselves as well as to others. To feel the loss of a strong sense of self—what the first division tries to guarantee and validate—means that we are suddenly brought closer than ever to the precarious nature of our own existence and the ways that we sovereignly construct our self-narratives. We often rest firmly in the belief that we are "such and such" when in fact we might just as easily become something quite different, something not so certain and secure, something incredibly vulnerable to those multiple external forces that lay along the edge of our existence (e.g., illnesses, betrayals, natural disasters, accidents, and so on).

Deliberately entering deeper into one's vulnerability and allowing one's identity to be divided further from within is not something to be avoided, however. It is rather the very means by which we come to value other humans and the rest of our world too. By accessing our most vulnerable space inside ourselves, one free of every attempt by us or others to label it, and so attempt to fully comprehend and control it, we are brought into closer proximity to others who have become acquainted, whether voluntarily or by force, with their own fragile existence. The only way to genuinely stand in solidarity with another, shoulder-to-shoulder, is to embrace one's own poverty. This, and nothing else, is what allows us to experience that meeting of two or more vulnerable selves in a state that we frequently call love.

Perhaps the sovereign self, as a redemptive, generative self, exhibits a sense of universal solidarity through a permanent encounter with weakness

21. See the series of arguments made throughout Hegel, *Science of Logic*.

and vulnerability, but it would have to be a self that knows it could always slide back in-between worlds and that no return to self is truly ever permanent.

Sovereignty, like those canonical, normative representational forms we shape and adhere to, presents itself as a necessary illusion in the sense that it is entirely fabricated by our own design, subject to innumerable criticisms, and yet it is something that we need so that we might ascribe order to our world. In other words, we cannot do without these sovereign gestures for they allow us to use things like language, to have order in our communities, and to identify who we are to ourselves and to others. Though we will have brilliant and perhaps also terrifying moments where we lose sight of each of these things in our lives, such as when our sense of self becomes rattled and ruined by a traumatic experience, we yet find a way to reinvent ourselves and reidentify ourselves once again. We would not be human unless we contained this radical propensity to recreate ourselves over and over again.

What this radical reinvention of the self points toward is the absolutely hollow nature of our existence, how there is really very little that uniquely characterizes us as human beings in distinction from those other animal species that lie all-too-close to us. We seem simply to be able to recognize that there is an emptiness at our core that allows for such radical reinventions of ourselves. We repeatedly harness that central emptiness in order to construct new images of ourselves throughout time. What makes us human is precisely the fact that we are able to use this internal abyss of meaning in order to produce incredibly creative measures. In many ways, our inability to exhaustively define ourselves is, in reality, our greatest gift in that it allows us to produce a near limitless number of artistic creations. This is the same thing as stating, as the Portuguese writer Fernando Pessoa once did, that it is our artificiality that is most natural to us.[22]

It is not just the realms of art or of personal identity that benefit from and are given life by the nothingness that swirls within us. The production of ideas themselves, these ephemeral and fleeting thoughts that flit through our brains, takes place each time as a moment of the individual human being confronting the empty space within—perhaps encountered externally as something like boredom—that yet has the power to transform the entirety of our materially embodied conditions. The simple deployment of an idea, in all its immaterial glory, is capable of altering political spheres, economic

22. Pessoa, *Book of Disquiet*.

conditions, agricultural developments, urban landscapes, technological progress, aesthetic enjoyment, and so much more.

The capacity to think thoughts, to embrace our inner potential and to recreate our actual lived existence based on nothing but a series of thoughts is the defining trait of our species. Because we can abstract ourselves from the immediacies of lived existence, like hunger and our exposure to the elements of nature, we are able to carve out a peculiar and unique life for ourselves unlike anything else this world had ever seen before.

Our empty core, which can never be filled, has brought about a history of religious questing to provide the sacred filling to our human donut hole, such as when Augustine once famously commented in his *Confessions* that our hearts are restless until they rest in God.[23] But perhaps there is nothing that goes within this hole, nothing to fill our longing or to permanently quell our sorrow. A dominant political theology is what takes shape when we suggest that something *can* fill this gap once and for all, and that nothing else will work. This is what happens when we speculate that something in our "nature" dictates that a particular positive redoubling is itself eternal— like that men should dominate over women, or that darker skinned persons are somehow inferior to lighter skinned individuals, and so on.

So how are we to perceive this ache that is a longing for what will always lie beyond us? What beatific union looks like, if one would stop to ask any mystic worthy of their salt, is more akin to what John of the Cross called a "dark night of the soul" wherein most of what we took to be the way we are or the way the world works is darkened to the point of being nearly effaced.[24] Coming into close proximity to the hollowness within, we can easily lose sight of our sense of all things sovereign, including ourselves.

Humans are actually getting closer to touching their nature when they drift into those negative zones within us where we encounter only our own uselessness, our lack of productivity, our ability to do nothing, our leisure time and ability to rest, our non-possessive and nonviolent sides, all of which call to mind the shutting down of the large machine that we other-wise usually identify with our busy lives and bodies.

In a philosophical register, we might say that when we render inopera-tive the mechanisms that typically generate our human nature, we discover that there is no nature beneath it all. This realization is precisely what makes us human.[25]

23. Augustine, *Confessions*.
24. John of the Cross, *Collected Works*.
25. See Agamben, *Open*.

This all makes a certain logical sense too, as we are most able to connect with others when we have no set goal, aim, or agenda, when we are literally willing to "waste time" with another person. These moments, which mainly take place when we are kids and truly have nothing better to do, are what foster stronger bonds than any scheduled activity intended to build group cohesiveness (unless that group building is intentionally aimed toward doing nothing in particular). This is how I would likewise define prayer, as a "waste of time" aimed at nothing more, but also nothing less, than building a relationship with the unknown and that which we do not understand—those contradictions that life forces us to confront, but never to resolve.

The intellectual life itself, one might argue, and as a recent writer has in fact argued, is a "useless" endeavor that actually cultivates the inner life and a sense of freedom that has the power, in turn, to radically alter our lives.[26] We should not be fooled by the lures of social status, political activism, or the superficiality of spectacles literally exploding before our eyes every day in our cultural and online personae. Taking the time to almost literally "do" nothing is the only thing that will actually bring about change in our personal lives and in our world. This is why any religious person should not shy away from admitting immediately and emphatically that prayer, because it aims for these things, is indeed a colossal waste of time, and that it should never seek to be productive or useful. To drift into that capitalist inspired efficiency-driven domain is to lose sight completely of what makes us most authentically human.

Human beings, because they have this unique capacity to generate ideas and thoughts from within the emptiness within themselves will always be able to establish a critical, inner voice—the conscience, as it has come to be called—that can radically call into question any external phenomena. The negative inclinations that we possess as innate characteristics of our humanity—our useless, unproductive, empty traits—are what give our existence a decidedly impoverished air. The poverty of being human, which draws us endlessly toward the vulnerable, the suffering, and those who are violently excluded from any group identity, is also our greatest asset. We resonate with that which we cannot possess precisely because we cannot possess it. And instead of trying to then possess the unpossessable, like the fools that we normally are, perhaps we can learn to see how it is only through our poverty and our inability to possess things, even our own selves and our stories about ourselves, that we might actually come to enjoy this life.

26. Hitz, *Lost in Thought*.

Take natural landscapes, for instance, which are something we cannot possess, but can only observe.[27] Stepping back on the edge of a precipice overlooking a deep canyon or standing at the summit of a giant mountain overlooking a vast wilderness evokes an experience of the sublime because it is something we cannot possess by any measure. Everything around us moves to its own music and there is nothing we can do to bring it under our control. Rather than intimidate us, as so many throughout history have experienced it and so tried to dominate it, such experiences of nature should be the very thing that draws us that much closer to our own nature, to the unpossessable abyss within us that yet defines us only as the undefinable creatures that we are.

The philosopher Giorgio Agamben has tried to give a description of what this inner freedom might look like when he depicts the "whatever being" (or "form-of-life" as he mainly calls it) that defies any category, label, or understanding that we might otherwise try to reduce it to. Whatever being is, for him, something we are all capable of living, a type of existence where we do not fit into a particular order and so we do not become violently reduced to whatever coordinates we usually use to classify people. We refuse to try and comprehend how they do or do not "fit in" within a given society. The "whatever being" lives beyond the normative order because it is uniquely attuned to the hollowness at its core, refusing to cover it over in an attempt to flee the anxiety that such a gaping hole within us might otherwise produce.

The "whatever being" is absolutely singular, something that cannot be compared to other beings. In truth, we can only experience intimacy with another once we let go of the standard relations that generally define our bonds with other humans—familial, religious, national. When we let go of such established relations and simply accept the undefined person who stands before us, and who acknowledges the emptiness within themselves just as we acknowledge the emptiness within ourselves, we are able to connect through our shared vulnerability and the admittance that we are often not who we claim to be. This act of mutual recognition is at times profound enough to undo the categories and labels that society has foisted upon us. So too is such a process able to see beyond the acts of marginalization and exclusion that mostly define our social and hierarchical worlds.

27. Agamben, *Use of Bodies.*

CHAPTER THREE

Haunting the Church

THE PROTESTANT THEOLOGIAN STANLEY Hauerwas has frequently repeated that his ecclesiology is one in which the church's priority is simply *to be the church*. This sovereign, tautological, and redoubled claim is imperative, he argues, so that the church might remain faithful to its narrative, to its virtuous living, and to its communal identity.[1] To be clear, this is more or less a robust but also entirely self-referential ecclesiology, one that might emphasize communitarian principles a bit too strongly, but which is also necessarily stated at some level for any communal identity to maintain itself.

The problem with such formulations, if taken to be the only guiding mandate for group identity, is what is to be done when the church, as it inherently always does, produces an element that is, as Rosemary Radford Ruether once put it, against itself?[2] From minority positions crying out to be heard to oppressed persons living in fear of pronouncing their so-called "deviant" or "heretical" identity to the community, what is the church to do with those living outside of its normative boundaries, whether in the form of other religious traditions or as those living unseen and unheard *within* the community?

For decades, contextual theologians have been outspoken on such issues, reframing the nature of ecclesiology to the point that many now understand that the church fails to be church when it is not attentive to the voices of those living on its own margins. The more recent efforts of queer theologians have even gone so far, on occasion, to question the very concept of normativity, rendering Christ's foundational gestures of grace as themselves antinomian in the sense of subverting whatever normative identity

1. See, among other places, Hauerwas, *The Hauerwas Reader*.
2. Ruether, *The Church Against Itself*.

we might wish to ascribe to "Christian" being.[3] But, then again, the communitarian might inquire, what is to become of the actual existing, institutionalized form of the church today—the one that, despite nondenominational efforts to meet in school buildings or community centers, often does have a building to maintain, tithes to collect, leadership to coordinate and gathered "Christians" to watch over?

Despite Kierkegaard's protest, nearly two centuries ago, that being a default member of Christendom caused one to bear the false moniker of "Christian," theologians are less poised than ever to give up this most fundamental of religious identifications.[4] The rest of our world, however, seems, conversely, more content than ever to relinquish any sense of being religious at all. The contrast between the orthodox and the heretical, for example, does not really concern many people today, those both internal and external to the church.

The claim that one belongs to a particular religious community and not another because an absolute truth is to be found only in their own backyard, is a claim that is generally founded upon a tautological proposition: I believe this community to be my access to truth because it shows me how to access the truth of my world. It is the same claim that is often made about divine revelation: I believe these claims to be divine in origin because the scriptures tell me that they are divine. What constitutes the "Barthian revolt" in modern theology, as Gary Dorrien has phrased the modern theological, defensive shift against the erosion of authority, is little more than a staunch allegiance to the tautological grounds of the Word of God as the justification for what ultimately cannot be justified: why I belong here, in this particular community, and not over there in another one.[5]

Because no community can exist as absolute, with therefore an unquestionable authority over its members, there must always be a contradiction at the heart of its own self-understanding. No matter how orthodox one tries to be in maintaining consistency in one's own self-perception, there will always be an internal element that serves to undermine one's claims to totality. Rather than grasp this dynamic as being itself foundational to our sense of identity on the whole, we instead exist as if the gap were insurmountable between the two opposing tensions. From political divisions between conservative and liberal to psychological dichotomies between the pleasure principle

3. Althaus-Reid, *Indecent Theology.*

4. Kierkegaard, *Attack upon "Christendom."*

5. Dorrien, *Barthian Revolt.*

and the death drive, we are repeatedly faced with competing forces whose relationship we have yet to fully understand. In ecclesial terms, this tension is not only locatable in those who would support reform versus those who would deny it, it is also the constitutive tension between the Kingdom of God and the all-too-earthly church.[6]

At the core of Judaism, no less, we find a propensity for unification and normative order in those positions that might be characterized as legalistic and those that appear to house a complete disdain for law, which are marked by a certain prophetic character, as I have already mentioned. This tension is never resolved within Jewish scripture, for example, though it is apparent that there is no way to reconcile the views of each. One cannot uphold Torah while also denying its force upon the community.

Taking note of this unresolvable duality between the legalistic and the prophetic within Jewish identity, especially as it was formulated in Paul Ricoeur's *The Symbolism of Evil*, eventually led me to formulate a more philosophical terminology for the same coupling: the canonical and the messianic.[7] Why pick such exalted and mysterious terms to replace a more biblical sounding pair? Mainly because these were the precise terms already being used by various European philosophers—such as Walter Benjamin, Jacques Derrida, and Giorgio Agamben, among others—to describe the same, or similar, dynamics at play within that precise biblical duality, and these more recent, philosophical terms were incredibly helpful to define what was really going on in a contemporary religious context, though no theologian seemed to be saying as much directly. This is, of course, how dissertations often get written, to explain how one thing that is going on over here is *very nearly the same thing* as what is going on over there.

The canonical impulse, to put things simply, is manifested any time an individual or a community tries to put a definitive stamp of approval on something as "the way it is," the way in fact things appear to *have* to be. Canonical forms therefore often run the risk of being accepted as sacred or a part of nature. Religious scriptures are often this very thing as well: a closed canon of texts that claim divine status precisely through their being "closed," or, not open to including any further revelations from on high because they already contain all that is needed. An "open" canon, in contrast, would be like the classics of western literature, where Plato and Shakespeare have dominated for centuries, though, these days, we are saying things like, "Why not Toni Morrison and James Baldwin, too?" and we are correct for suggesting such additions because an open canon is always in need of updating to

---

6. See Congar, *True and False Reform*.

7. See my *Between the Canon and the Messiah*; as well as Ricoeur, *Symbolism of Evil*.

include those who had previously, for whatever reason, been left out. The voices that are often heard most loudly are those in positions of privilege and power, in need of being haunted by those other voices repressed or ignored for far too long.

Whenever an identity, a community's sense of who it is to itself, a definition, an argument, or the like, is definitively nailed down once and for all, you enter into a canonical framework that attempts to give a permanence or absoluteness to something that, most likely, cannot be made so permanent, or seemingly eternal. You attempt to provide the sheen of being historically transcendent to something that is, in reality, far more dependent upon contingent circumstances.

Whenever a canon becomes too "fixed" as it were, attempting to appear as eternal and unchanging (or as utterly "natural," as some would opine), we can rest assured that someone will rise up from some quarter and begin the revolutionary process of calling the entire canon into question. These deconstructive forces are referred to as messianic because they will come like the Messiah was expected to come and so correct what had been blown far off its intended course. The fantasy that such a messianic corrective would be once and for all is what often prevents us from accepting the fact that the church, like its doctrine, can and does change over time, as John Henry Newman once soundly demonstrated.[8] This dynamic is the force that once prompted the philosopher Jacques Derrida to make it abundantly clear that his version of messianic forces would never be historically embodied in an actual messianic figure, for then justice would feign to be complete, or more likely, it would seek to embody a corrupt and impossible totalitarian gesture.[9]

The messianic is rather the still small voice, the marginalized or repressed force, that gathers itself within every canonical form, crying out to be heard and wanting desperately for each particular canon to be adjusted so that they no longer push certain elements to the periphery but acknowledge them, recognize them, as central to their own, ever-expanding identities. It might be simplest to say that, every time an identity becomes too rigid or too inflexible, certain messianic voices will appear on the horizon declaring that an injustice has been done in preventing their appearance. For this reason, violence becomes a major index of measuring just how fixed certain canonical norms are; are we willing to repress those who appear as different, divergent, or even opposed to the governing norms of a society,

8. See Newman, *Essay on the Development*.
9. Derrida, *Specters of Marx*.

or are we willing to embrace their criticisms of the normative order, adapt and change our ways so that we might evolve and grow into something new?

It should be no surprise that those communities that feel threatened or resentful of having lost something are those often most willing to enact violent measures in order to shore up a uniform identity for themselves and for many unwilling others. From fascist political regimes to religious fundamentalists, we see such tactics repeatedly on display throughout modern history. When we see Black Lives Matter protestors today, or anyone who attempts to speak on behalf of a community that has felt severely restrictive forces belaboring them in one form or another, we must be attentive to these larger processes that refuse to go away once and for all. Making the argument that a historically contingent Messiah has eradicated all need for this dynamic to be acknowledged and maintained is a recipe for politically totalitarian forms—something with which the church is unfortunately all too familiar.

We are, all of us, caught somewhere in-between a fixed sense of ourselves and those isolated, repressed, traumatized, or marginalized voices within us that are trying to poke their heads into the light of day. Whether we recognize, or are conscious of, this state of affairs, however, is another matter altogether.

It is somewhat of a truism to suggest that the main difference between the orthodox believer and their counterpart, the heretic, at least in historical terms, lies in who was able to successfully grasp power at a given time in history—that is, who was able to decide upon what was to be considered "orthodox" in the first place. History, as we well know, is quite often written by those in positions of both power and privilege who are able to dictate the "story" of a nation, a religion, a people, or an event in ways that conform with their general worldview. This has been the case within a number of contexts, from communist countries to nations wishing to conceal past genocides. Indeed, as R. I. Moore has recently demonstrated in his survey of this division in his book *The War on Heresy*, most often throughout the centuries, people or groups were labeled as "heretical" not because they simply deviated from a standard teaching or belief, but because a particular political and cultural authority had to be asserted and extended, and they were the people who stood in its way.[10]

It is true, of course, that many persons silenced as such by the "official" narrative of history were often the oppressed group, and so, for that very

10. Moore, *War on Heresy*.

reason, their stories often contained a good deal of truth about what was actually going on in matters of fact (e.g., slave narratives on oppression or Native American mistreatment at the hands of European colonizers). This is one of the reasons, moreover, that Howard Zinn's book *A People's History of the United States* has been so popular over the years, as he confirms the necessity for an "alternate" account of US history in order to demonstrate how the version of history many received in school was not the only, or even best, version of events.[11] This is also the power we feel latent behind Clint Eastwood's film *Letters from Iwo Jima*, which dares to deliver to an American audience the Second World War in the Pacific from a Japanese perspective.

I mention such stories to make a point that needs to be made and then repeated: we often discuss things in easily comprehensible terms so that we can readily make sense of them, even when the reality we live in is far more complex and far more deserving of further nuance and inquiry. We simplify in order to represent when the events or people represented are actually impossible to represent in any completely accurate way. The only accurate representation we can give of something is to demonstrate our failure to project a perfect representation, not to actually create a truly, authentically "accurate" portrait, as philosophers have noted.[12] In making our representations, however, we often also miss the fact that our imposed categories and definitions are capable of misrepresentation as well.

There are many times when we talk about faith or theology in broad metaphysical terms, for example, when we are really talking about politics, and the boundaries and borders we find useful and authoritative in *this* world. In our frequently conjured portrayals of the afterlife, we do not like to imagine someone on the other side of the fence in this world ending up in the same place we are for eternity, and so we divide things up into believers and nonbelievers, orthodox and heretic, the saved and the damned, as only a few such examples among the many that frequently shade our pictures of religious belief. The "us" and "them" mentality that defines political interaction therefore becomes easily applicable to religious teachings when we strive to see these borders extended into the afterlife.

It is a sad commentary on our failure to think beyond our allegedly metaphysical context when we realize, as some have suggested, that there is a direct correlation between cultural perceptions of the "necessary" punishments for sin and our inability to rehabilitate criminals within a given society. The heaven/hell dichotomy, one might say, is really about the pleasure

---

11. Zinn, *People's History of the United States*.
12. Both Judith Butler and Giorgio Agamben have repeatedly made this point.

one takes in maintaining an absolute justification, so as to have a "clean conscience," for dealing out severe punishments, such as solitary confinement, cruel and torturous prison conditions, and capital punishment. As Phil Zuckerman has noted, this is why religious countries typically avoid talk about rehabilitation in favor of a pseudo-religious legitimation for punishing criminals as their God presumably would.[13]

Politics, like those that surround incarceration tactics in heavily religious countries, revel in simplistic representations that appear as fundamental beliefs which suggest a sort of eternality, but are supposed to address the practical material before our very noses. Political parties talk in terms of absolute values when what we really need are far more mundane decisions to be made in order to pass legislation designed to have practical outcomes. Shorn of the absoluteness of metaphysical foundations for our positions, we might actually be more open to alternative formulations that, in reality, work much better, more humanely, and more reasonably.

I would only suggest that in matters of faith, historically speaking at least, we have also often formulated abstractions concerning the nature of the eternal (e.g., God as "all powerful," "all knowing," etc.), and have likewise overlooked the mundane in search of the absolute. The same questions we might put to politicians in this regard might also be put to people of faith: why must God be seen this way? To protect God's power? Or are we really seeking to preserve the power that humans often claim to have in relation to such a mighty deity?

Whether such abstract thoughts on the divine are the actual focus that religion should take is the main question, and one that contains significant implications for why a person is a member of a religious community at all. For, as many atheist positions have made clear more recently, there is no way to justify one's belonging in a particular community over any other community, unless one feels that a given community somehow maintains an absolute claim upon them that another community cannot replicate, some certain and undeniable truth that undergirds one's fidelity to that particular community and no other.

Social order; a solid sense of oneself and one's identity; the functioning of memory, rationality, and logic; the boundaries of any community—these things are all built upon canonical acts of exclusion, though we rarely think of them that way. If we don't listen to the excluded others among us, living in nearly every corner of every society on this planet, we end up sacralizing,

---

13. Zuckerman, *What It Means to Be Moral*, 252–53.

naturalizing, and fetishizing the structures and normative identities that shape our lived and embodied identities, that guide us and help us to communicate with each other, *but do not actually define us in any exhaustive sense*. We are capable of transcending any definition placed upon us by ourselves or by others, though we are also deeply indebted to the definitions of ourselves that we create.

The human being, as many philosophers have noticed, has generally been defined as the only creature capable of recognizing itself *as* a human being.[14] Though this may turn out someday to not actually be true—who knows if dolphins or elephants can't do the same thing, and recognize themselves *as* dolphins or elephants, albeit differently than we do—we do frequently insist on subordinating ourselves to the labels and categories that we construct in order to assert our sovereignty over every other living creature.

This task we embrace of defining our uniqueness among the rest of the animal kingdom is really a reflection of the same methods we employ when entering into community with fellow humans. To be a part of a community is to know one's stories as separate from other stories, and thus to have boundaries and borders of some kind. To have an operational memory, we must forget things or be cursed to remember everything and so be paralyzed by the weight of a comprehensive history. To have any sense of order at all, one must eliminate, or at least marginalize, anything that seems "chaotic" to the functioning of the system, even if, a while later, one is able to incorporate some of those so-called "chaotic" elements into the normative dimensions of a given order. This is the cost of definition itself, hence of having language. Though we would so often like to think that we can create a world free from all acts of exclusion, this is a utopian dream that would actually turn into a nightmare should it be realized.

For the philosopher Paul Ricoeur, to have a "happy memory" means that one *must* forget things, though one must also be able to "happily" recall whatever one has forgotten and so seemingly left in the past.[15] This means that any repressed, violent, or traumatic memories must be addressed, perhaps even faced for the first time, so that an individual can work toward the cultivation of a happy memory and not simply maintain one that is stressed or otherwise unnaturally altered. Memory, just like the histories that permeate every culture, is an organic process that is neither perfect nor unnecessary. Though we would like to have photographic memories that could retain the finest detail of whatever it is we seek to recall, the truth is that

14. This claim is studied in depth in Agamben, *Open*.
15. Ricoeur, *Memory, History, Forgetting*, 496–503.

such a memory, if lasting and fixed forever, would be a source of torment and a justification for being incredibly inflexible, perhaps even unforgiving.

René Girard, one of the most intriguing of writers concerning the nature of exclusion, mythology, and cultural memory, has cautioned us against sacralizing a particular narrative of exclusion because the odds are high that doing so means we are concealing a violence that goes unnamed at the heart of our social relations. He defines mythology, in fact, as the act of covering up violent acts of exclusion, and he looks to the ways that scriptures from around the world work to uncover violence and denounce it.[16] This is not to suggest that we can simply do away with all forms of violence once and for all. Rather, Girard wanted humanity to become more aware of how violence permeates nearly every facet of our lives and that, by recognizing this reality, we might be able to do a better job at lessening the hold of violence over us.

One of the greatest temptations that humanity has undergone in facing this particular dualistic tension between canonical norms and their messianic undoing is that we have often labeled and resisted the latter force as nothing but a foreign element within an otherwise holy alliance of like-minded souls. So many heretics, deviants, so-called "perverts" and other differently minded individuals or groups have been targeted as divergences from the system too great for the system—any cohesive and coherent system really—to bear. Because there is a tendency in the messianic to call into question the entire canonical form, such "weak" forces, as they are sometimes called, are often taken to be opposed to canonical forms altogether.[17] To label these forces as antinomian, or opposed to *all* law, as if they were calling for a nihilistic end to all recognized forms of representation (like language itself, for example) is to miss the point that every messianic force arises from *within* the canonical measure, as a part of it that cannot simply be effaced once and for all.

As in the modern period where we see those who fear any challenge to the ruling order as a nihilistic assault on "real" values and traditions that might lead to an inevitable decline to any sense of identity altogether, there is no way to actually live out an antinomian existence. As any student of psychology will tell you, we all need a solid sense of self in order to function at all in this world, even if our sense of self is an illusion that we are using to prop up an insecure ego, leaving us in need of a major realignment in our

16. Girard, *I See Satan Fall Like Lightning.*

17. See the dialogue between René Girard and Gianni Vattimo as published by Antonello, ed., *Christianity, Truth, and Weakening Faith.*

sense of who we are to ourselves. We likewise need language to be able to communicate effectively with one another, even if the language we rely on needs to be updated so as to be less offensive to certain persons or groups.

I think here too of those political theorists today who call for more political representation, even voting rights for the natural world through human representatives, including all animal and insect species, as well as the water, air, and earth.[18] Though the obvious first reaction of many might be to dismiss such possibilities as "the end" of politics as we know it, which is usually based on the idea of human-only representation in our legislative bodies, the truth is that politics "as we know it" would survive in some altered form should we adapt enough to allow those creatures we are endangering and rapidly obliviating to have some much needed political representation and its accompanying power.

What all of this means is basically that every time an individual or some group of individuals cries out about how much injustice is being done to them because they have been ignored or pushed to the fringes of society, they might (metaphorically) be the voice of the Messiah crying out for justice in the wilderness, letting us all know that something is amiss and in need of correction. We need to start tracking the effectiveness of canonical measures, and the religions that often form and protect them by sacralizing what is otherwise contingent, by the violence they do to their marginalized elements rather than by their own internal claims to be divinely inspired. When someone objects to this suggestion by saying that there can be no objective, neutral standpoint from which to judge whether or not a particular canon is or is not violent, then I will continue to reassert the only criteria by which we *may* in fact judge them: how closely does one listen to *its own* internal, marginalized voices? If they do well at this, then I suspect the violence is less; if they do poorly, then we might consider them more willing to engage in violent actions aimed at maintaining systemic oppressions.

And what about those who like the ruling order because they receive privileges and benefits from it? Do we simply let them wither up and die so that a new system of privileges might bestow its favor upon a new class of persons? Isn't someone always going to dominate over someone else? Why should anyone be willing to part with the benefits that have been given to them anyway?

If pressed for it, this is the fear many privileged persons harbor, whether they say it out loud or not. For them, such nihilistic forces are to be resisted at every turn. Seriously examining how these questions should be

---

18. See, among others, the call for a "parliament of things" in Latour, *We Have Never Been Modern*.

addressed, or even broached, within an ecclesial context is therefore a very difficult thing for some to do. But doing so is also a simple way to ascertain the willingness of a given religious community to self-reflexively evaluate its propensity to silence its internal dissent, often through various forms of intimidation and violence.

The majority of philosophical and theological authors I study seem intent, not on understanding the nature and function of such dualistic tensions themselves—and therefore learning to see beyond one's myopic and often ideological worldview—but on aligning a particular configuration of concepts on only one side of the dualism. Clearly this is done to shore up a specific view of one's own world, and it is often conducted with deep and lasting political, economic, communal, cultural, and religious consequences.

When a theologian argues for a wholly transcendent deity who exists in immaterial form; is entirely autonomous and sovereign in their power; who dictates by necessity a particular predestined plan for everything that exists; who places clear borders and boundaries on all given identities; who defends a particular, moralistic vision of nature (or natural law); and who defends the traditions and values of a community because the status quo has so much worth preserving, I generally know that I am listening to a privileged individual, usually a man. The slightly distant and deistic vision of God that they champion is often little more than a mirroring of a detached father figure so many lament as a presence lost to their lives.

When a theologian, on the contrary, argues for an immanent model of God who exists in the materiality and bodies of all that has been created, dwells as an interdependent being who shares with the suffering of others, who recognizes the contingency of existence, welcomes porous boundaries and hybrid identities that seem to defy the laws of nature, but actually follow an evolution of natural processes, who does not proscribe moral norms but looks to the specific standpoint from which a person speaks and who respects the plurality of so many different communities that abound in our world, I generally know that I am hearing the voice of someone less privileged, probably a woman or a minority figure, someone more open to the differences that surround them and less inclined to promote a homogenous sense of sameness that governs the former's outlook on life. The slightly pantheistic model of God they often work with is in direct tension with any transcendent-deistic depiction of divine being, and maternal imagery often begins to abound in their descriptions of divine-human interaction.

These sketches are obviously reductive of the fuller visions given by so many diverse voices out there, and yet a kernel of truth remains in their respective emphases. To be fair, both energies are needed at times to sustain the communities and identities that exist in so many varied forms on this planet: we need those who seek to preserve what is good in what has already been established and we need those to point out what we have overlooked that might be hurting someone typically both unseen and unheard.

Yet it is comical, despite also being entirely tragic, how infrequently we stop to take note of the necessity for both voices to be heard. We often get caught up listening only to the extremists on either side, the concepts and worlds they create in order to then defend, and so we do not spend enough time noting the core dynamics that motivate both sides. Respect for the processes of preservation and maintenance of a community's values is only matched by an equal respect for those voices crying out for more justice from among the marginalized elements within a given community. Every community will always have such elements, and so it is well beyond time that we learned how to deal more practically with their existence and integration into whatever society we are talking about at a given point in history, on whatever surface of this globe.

Because we have labored for far too long with only one side dominating the game—the masculine, sovereign, transcendent, autonomous figure of power making absolute claims about divine and human existences—it is no surprise that many are loathe to relinquish the models of privilege and power that have constructed so many institutions and societal structures over the centuries. But the days of such supremacies are fading quickly, and for the better.

Finding balance between these dualistic impasses is that much more difficult because looking for "very fine people on both sides" can often be a rallying cry for tolerating some extreme members on one side and downplaying the cries for injustice on the other, as Donald Trump made abundantly clear in his remarks following the murder of a young woman by a white nationalist at the white supremacist rally in Charlottesville, Virginia, in 2017.

The impasses we often see, and exacerbate, between these two sides are not easy to discern in their core form. We often get caught up speaking in two different registers of discourse, and so basically speaking two different languages to each other while missing the point of why certain positions seem not only defensible but as the only realistic option to those who hold them.

We might take, for example, the tension between evolution and creationism that continues to haunt theological debate in certain quarters. This tension gets ignored in other settings altogether but is generally misunderstood entirely.

I recall some years ago being shown a tattoo on a gentleman's arm that contained a biblical reference to God creating the world. This tattoo was, for this particular person, "my little 'F' you to Darwin," as he so eloquently described it to me. The reason for such an objection to evolution was apparent in this individual's essential theological point of view. God, to be God, must be sovereign and autonomous, and therefore at the head of the family as much as the community. To be autonomous, for God as for a nation-state, as for a man, means to have no one telling them what to do, as this would compromise one's ability to function independently and therefore to be in complete control of themselves and their world. Theologically, such efforts result in the notion of creation *ex nihilo*, or "from nothing," a position that isn't actually in the Protestant Bible he reads, but which easily follows from subsequent philosophical speculation on the sovereignty and autonomy of divine being.

If something else precedes you, as with one's parents who give birth to you, then you are dependent upon them. If something came before God, then God would be dependent on that something else. The only thing that can come before our world and its creation, then, must be God—otherwise God would be dependent on something else and we would have to then worship that something else as the even higher "higher power." Defending God's ability to create the world is an act intended to defend God's sovereignty, which is based on God's autonomy and independence.

What is really transpiring in such defenses, however, is a robust projection of the community's right to be itself autonomous, not dependent on any evolutionary process describing what came before the community's foundation. In truth, there is no justification possible for a community to exist instead of some other community. The borders and boundaries, symbols, myths, and identities that make up the community are really no better, nor no worse, than any other community and we all sort of know this to be the case, inside religious circles and outside of them as well. There is just no legitimation of a particular community other than "this is my community and I love it because I belong here." And because our ability to defend our community is no stronger than our ability to defend our loyalty to a specific sports team, we rely upon preposterous defenses—what I'm going to call "necessary illusions"—in order to feel settled and "at home" in the places that we choose to reside.

The kicker here is that these necessary illusions are in point of fact both illusions, totally fabricated, *but also totally necessary*, because that's how communal identity and allegiance works. We need to maintain an idealistic perception of where we feel most like we belong because that's part of being human. It's how falling in love works too, when we romanticize our beloved as the perfect human being even though they have faults aplenty. When we fall in love, however, it is as if nothing preceded our love, as if nothing could take precedence over this specific love in our lives, as if destiny itself brought us together, which is a myth, or a lie that we tell ourselves, and yet this is precisely what we have to do in order to feel at home in the love that is being fostered between persons. As crazy as it sounds, I can know logically that there are many other people out there whom I could've also fallen in love with, but once I find "the one," I will retroactively view my relationship to them as if it were fated to happen in just the way it did.

On the other side of things, you have those wonderfully scientific-minded individuals who simply look at the creationists and think they are staring straight at the most ignorant people they have ever seen. How in the world could these overly simplistic dupes ignore the facts of evolution-ary theory and espouse such nonsense as that the world was created by a divine being in the sky, in complete defiance of biological, geological, and anthropological evidence that our world just kind of contingently happened the way it happened, no master plan required?

The obvious and outstanding merit of this search for scientific fact is only matched by the often accompanying and typically stunning lack of un-derstanding as to what really motivates a creationist's frustration with Dar-win's suggestions about the origins of humanity. To respond to a creationist's rebuttals and "evidence" with more scientific claims, as rock-solid and ac-curate as they generally can be, is to miss the entire point of the creationist's position. Presenting the fullness of evolutionary theory as a response to creationist claims is a woefully inadequate one that does not actually take account of what is at stake in the conversation.

Community, whether national, cultural, linguistic, family-oriented, politi-cal, religious, sports-based, or as it comes in basically any shape or size, is perhaps the best and most familiar way that we achieve a sense of identity. We exist in relation to other people and it is mostly in the ways in which oth-ers address us, teach us, and guide us that we come to know something of who we are. The moral life we live, with the virtues and values that we hold dear, derive from our placement within a collective grouping. Community is where we learn how to behave, essentially how to live, and there is no substitute for the warm embrace that a sense of belonging can bring.

When you find yourself immersed in a foreign context, not quite "at home" in the world, it usually has to do with the fact that you have entered into an uncomfortable place of unfamiliarity with the community around you. There is an awkwardness that accompanies having to locate yourself among people you are less familiar with and who might, by their very presence, challenge the way in which you orient yourself in the world. To be among those who practice different customs, speak a different language, hold different traditions and beliefs, or who simply look very different than you do, is to be forced *to see oneself as the foreign element*, as that which does not quite fit in. Unless one has a strong sense of self that can weather such storms, one can be more inclined to flee such scenes rather than face, or even realign, their identity to reflect the community around them. But, of course, this is what every community essentially asks you to do when you enter into it: to conform to its way of being or to go to another community and see if they accept you as you might, in turn, accept them. Unless there are obvious markers such as the violence a community tolerates that should not be tolerated, there's usually no solid way to legitimate your belonging to any one particular community over any other one.

Of course, it can also be the case that you feel like you don't fit in even with your home community. The problem with having a strong communal identity, in fact, is that a difficulty often arises when such a strong sense of self has to confront those who are within the same community but who don't hold or adhere to that same sense of self. From "fair weather fans" of a sports team to "real Americans" to "cafeteria Catholics," so many defenders of a strong communal identity have come up with various ways to label and dismiss the "heretics" within their bubble. The "black sheep" of many families are all-too-well acquainted with the aggressions, both large and small, that communal identities can manifest when they fear their values are being ignored, disrespected, or dismissed altogether.

It's nice to think that a person who disagrees with a particular community's way of being in the world—with the values it holds, its history, its traditions, or its habits—can just simply pick up and join a new one, like all those liberals who threaten to move to Canada when the wrong candidate in the United States wins a national election. And, certainly, there is a truth to this fantasy: you can leave a community and join up with another, becoming their adopted child. But there will be costs, of course, and losses to bear. It is also true that we are often much more invested in our communities than we realize, so that when we attempt to leave, we find it so much more difficult to do so than we had expected.

A person can be very tempted to align themselves with a strong sense of communal identity because it allows you to feel like you belong, to know exactly who you are and to abandon those nagging doubts about all the ways in which you might not fit in as well as you would like to. A community can also channel our resentments, anger, and grievances as well as our joys. A collective sense of well-being can place the guardrails firmly in place and prevent violence from spiraling out of control in many cases too.

It is clear that you can seek strong communities to be a part of and reinforce your sense of self blindly, with no regard for minorities within your own community, and this can lead to fascist political forms in the extreme. But it can also be awesome to just feel part of the community. Every community throughout history has its unhappy minorities who feel (and are) unrecognized and unheard to a greater or lesser degree. This is the uncomfortable reality of community life.

It can be terribly difficult, in fact, to face the reality that every community will displace, marginalize, or downplay certain voices. A healthy, functional community is one that is open to hearing its minority voices, whereas an unhealthy, repressive one closes itself off to such marginalized figures. But every community does have its marginal elements, and so it can be very easy for someone to get swept up in the feeling of belonging and miss out on the ways that a particular minority of persons isn't heard as clearly as they should be. Too many liberals miss this very point when they take an extreme position on impossible policies of radical inclusion, and which only angers those people who are trying to conserve their community's traditions and values.

I often wonder, though, if there is another way to belong to a community that might defy this dualistic impasse between the left and the right. And this "third way" is what I find when I look to Paul's writings on communal identity, something I can easily imagine being translated into a secular framework.

Pauline philosophy dictates that you need neither strongly identify with your communal identity nor oppose or abandon it. It is not a problem, of course, to love your community and its roots. Paul was himself quite capable of taking pride in his own Jewish heritage. But, as his life choices dictated, he also had little problem with subverting the typical identity formations associated with a given community, though without leaving them behind altogether either. He introduced a strange logic that we are still trying to get our heads around, one that may appear to many to be some form of relativism, but which allowed him to demonstrate a particular communal identity while also being willing to hold it lightly in his hands.

As I mentioned earlier, but which I want to elaborate in more detail here, Paul's claim was that his newfound freedom in Christ meant that he could subvert the strong claims of communal identity while at the same time outwardly appearing to adhere to them. He contended that he could be a Jew with other Jews and a Gentile with other Gentiles, though, to be clear, this logic would've entailed breaking a number of very important social rules and taboos associated with each group (e.g., think of his eating non-kosher foods, but then keeping a kosher diet when with the Jews, like passing for a vegetarian with the vegetarians, but then eating meat when you aren't with them, which might incur the ire of the vegetarians at some point).

Shouldn't one criticize Paul precisely because he seems to not take seriously the identity of the community? Indeed, what exactly was the community supposed to be if being a follower of Christ essentially meant being able to move so deftly between different, already existing communities? Could such a follower of Christ act comparably today like a Christian when with Christians, a Muslim when with Muslims, and an atheist when with the atheists?

What Paul basically did was to locate a weakness within the strong identity that is actually a new type of strength, as it allowed him to go between communities and share their values when with them. He was able to do this because he recognized that one's spirit and one's flesh don't fully coincide. A gap remains between them that makes possible the oscillations we recognize as those representations we give of ourselves and which are prone to numerous changes throughout our lifetime. Admitting that they don't entirely coincide is what allows for the recognition that our identity can be undone. Trying to say that one's flesh and spirit do coincide, fully, without remainder, is actually something closer to becoming a totalizing or totalitarian gesture. It is only in something like a fascist context that one would claim to fully identify with the community's representations of itself—something that is in reality impossible to do.

Likewise, as with flesh and spirit, grace and law don't fully coincide either, and so we return to this fundamental theological problem again and again: the prophetic versus the legalistic, freedom versus determination, contingency versus necessity, peace versus violence, and so on. Each of these tensions is really one between language (as law) and experience (as grace, or freedom). We are bound by forces that constrain us, but which also give us the power to communicate with one another and to be in community with each other. We will always transcend language, experiencing things that we just can't put into words, and yet we will always return to language because we need to use it to establish any semblance of order and mutual understanding.[19]

When we cease simply trying to adhere to one side in a dualistic impasse, we might be able to note that learning to respond to both sides as a necessary ebb and flow of human life means that it will always appear as if there is an excessive quality to whatever existence we are living. Because we must always find a way to take up both claims at the same time, though each side seeks to attend to the representations and discourses that comprise only one, partial perspective on reality. Hence, our world always appears—in whatever reductive form we view it—as if there were more to reality than we can see, as if reality itself were "not all" there was to reality.[20]

It is easy to see why those communities that seek to ground what is ultimately without a ground end up making abstract and absolute metaphysical claims about their own foundations. This is traditionally the domain of the metaphysical, taken as the bedrock of the religious, and it is the main way that we have historically come to imagine our sense of belonging to a particular religious community.

The riches of our imaginations are, however, left to wander and roam throughout the gaps that exist between our experiences and the limits of representation that we constantly encounter, whether in language, art, music, our politically creative solutions, and so forth. Though we might be tempted to locate divine being within the infinite play that takes place between our finite representations, it is really our inability to suture the split between the spirit and the flesh, the rich interplay of metaphor not metaphysics, that constantly redetermines our perceptions of reality.

From time to time, we grow impatient and frustrated with the limitations that language and community impose upon us, and so we seek out totalitarian or utopian solutions that strive to completely eradicate the disjunction, only to realize that these fantasies are ultimately unsustainable or even horrifically violent. Learning to see the reality of the dualistic impasses themselves means learning to see the reality of our social formations themselves anew.

19. This commentary on Pauline thought is indebted to the one offered by Agamben, *Time that Remains*.

20. There is an obvious affinity here with the ontology offered routinely by Slavoj Žižek, such as in his *Less Than Nothing*.

So, when we want to discern more clearly what a proper ecclesiology is or could be, what theory of community seems best to legitimate what ultimately can never be legitimated, we must begin to ask more fundamental questions about why we are seeking to develop such theories in the first place, what power and privileges we are seeking to maintain.

Some years ago, I stumbled across a fascinating thesis on the nature of fetishism in the modern period: that our theories about the fetish, which are abundant and often in contradiction with one another, are really a proxy conversation about our fetish for theory.[21] In the absence of one universal and absolute position on the nature of our material embodiment, such as premodern religious views mainly provided, we moderns create and cling to multiple competing theories on the immanent transcendence of materiality itself in order to address what cannot really be addressed: the uncertainty and discomfort of our having the wholly immanent bodies that we nonetheless constantly long to transcend.

As Eric Santner has shown, we take great pleasure in our ability to theorize because this is where we locate something of the absoluteness that religion once demanded from itself, but which has mainly vacated our collective, modern world.[22] It is no wonder that ecclesiology is a distinctively modern project for this is the time period in which the crisis of authority has taken place, and in which we feel an increased desperation to defend the indefensible. If premodern theologies were more concerned about finding enjoyable theories regarding God's existence in order to legitimate miserable human existences, it makes sense that modern theological inquiries, facing an onslaught of plurality, multiple-belongings, and hybrid identities, would focus on what makes belonging to this community more distinct than belonging to any other.

Perhaps it will eventually be shown to be the case that defending a utopian vision of the Kingdom of God in tension with the political realities of the church will be a suitable, even beneficial model for an ecclesial community to thrive. In the face of utopian thought, which is necessary to imagine for any real change to take place in our world, it will also, no doubt, be a laboratory for new political forms of association and representation that we have yet to conceive. Even bolder still, perhaps we simply need to recognize that all of us—those within church and those outside of it—are caught within the same unending dynamics and need to admit as much in order to move forward, together.

21. Böhme, *Fetishism and Culture*.
22. Santner, *Untying Things Together*.

CHAPTER FOUR

Haunting Our Words

THE GAP THAT EXISTS between the spirit and the flesh is in fact the same gap that exists between the thing itself and the word we use to describe it. In this space that forever separates the object we look at and our symbols or representations of the very same object—what fills up our languages with the many words we use to describe reality "in the flesh" so to speak—we encounter a distance that can never be bridged. Though we continuously desire to shape our words in such a way so as to more fully and accurately describe reality, we can never exhaustively accomplish this task. Our words fail us repeatedly because they can never become one with the object or experience they are trying to describe.[1] This gap is how all language works, but it is also how all identities work too, and it is the religious way of being in the world that has traditionally safeguarded the processes of identity formation through language.

It should be no surprise that religions, those that have lasted throughout the centuries, have a unique relationship to a particular language and the community that speaks it. The Word itself, especially in the monotheistic traditions of the West, becomes the unique bearer of divine revelation, often causing a contingent linguistic experience to become enshrined within the tradition. The Hebrew of the Jews, the Latin of western then Catholic Christendom, the Arabic of the Qur'an—these languages bear the weight of the divine Word and they have been revered and preserved because they attempt to capture best an ultimately unpresentable reality.

Language and religion work seemingly hand-in-hand to bring personal and communal identities into being. They in fact contain an immediate similarity in that they both focus on symbols and symbolic statements. In

1. See Dickinson, *Words Fail.*

this sense they both constitute a large network of interwoven symbols that are passed on from generation to generation. They are both "deep structures" that run across human societies and both contribute principally to the formation of any given communal culture, as they are taught to children who consequently find it hard to ever fully depart from the language or religion (or lack of religion) of their childhood. In fact, both seem to be universal to humanity, geographically and historically.

Each language, like every religion, is more or less a "closed" system of reference. Language regulates the functioning of a particular body of persons who speak this specific dialect. And in order for it to function, it must "forget" its past, or what we would consider to be the obvious influences of other languages upon it. No language stands permanently fixed, yet every dictionary or grammar book presents itself as if this were the case. Knowing the origins of a language is not necessary in order for it to function in its present. Moreover, for people to be able to understand each other, there are certain "rules" that need to be more or less adhered to. These rules, however, as a good scholar of linguistics would note, almost always have exceptions, and some are maintained and taught despite being unnecessary. The infractions of straining a preposition or splitting an infinitive are remnants of the Latin language, and essentially not necessary for the English language in order to convey the clarity of meaning of a given expression. Yet there are many grammarians who cling to such rules as if they define the "civilized" nature of the culture brought about through a specific language. What is obviously true is that a language must have a certain shared set of norms that regulate its usage and guarantee the language's intelligibility for a specific group of people. We must therefore have teachers of grammar.

In religious terms, these guardians would be the doctrinal systems upheld and taught by the catechists, priests, and even bishops, who articulate a shared system of dogmatic meaning for their people. It would make a certain sense then why these two groups have a typical hesitancy to embrace any "hasty" changes to the norms that secure meaning for a group of persons. This situation would also serve to explain why any changes that do happen take so long to spread out to the people.

In truth, many changes actually proceed in reverse, with the practices of the people changing first and only later being "officially" accepted by those who "govern" the norms, whether this is the case with new words being eventually accepted by dictionary makers, accepted linguistic practices eventually being adopted by grammarians or popular religious practices eventually becoming doctrinal propositions accepted by a religious institution. History bears out these examples in abundance.

Upon closer inspection, language turns out to be highly fluid, an ever-changing practice that includes many exceptions. Religion, for its part, turns out to be just as fluid, even when it claims not to be. Those who study such systems closely, the linguists and theologians among us, will tell us that changes do happen, and often, though the "closed" nature of these respective systems tempts us again and again to "forget" about these outside influences and to proceed as if the system has always functioned this way (e.g., the "foreign" word becomes part of our language, the "foreign" religious belief becomes part of a new belief system, etc.).

This context calls to mind the popularized notion of having to learn the grammatical rules before you can break them, as "good writers" often do. What does this adage say about religious views? Should we learn them well in order to later "break" them in the sense that we accept deviation as part of the evolving nature of linguistic and religious practices? This would seem to be a natural part of practicing a given system such as language or religion. Yet it is also the most difficult to "define" (or accept) precisely because it will not be recognized as integral to the operations of a given "closed system" of reference (i.e., a "closed" canonical norm).

Here there is perhaps a difference between language and religion. Languages are more "open" as they evolve based on usages (i.e., dictionaries are updated, grammar guides and spellings change), while religions with closed scriptures appear not as readily amended—though this may also not be entirely the case, as the frameworks through which we interpret scriptures do continuously change. Our understanding of slavery, for example, has altered the way in which we read scriptural passages about slavery. What we witness again and again is the difficulty of ascertaining how a scriptural pronouncement becomes a culturally accepted practice, or a doctrine itself.

Related to these thoughts, we should also consider the role of metaphor in the establishment of both definitions of things and doctrines specifically. How is something that is only analogous to something else ("the sun is a red disc") able to become a doctrine? The question this is asking is: how is a biblical-literary story able to dictate something of the reality of our world? Or, again, concerning language: how is this word, this concept, able to depict something of our reality, what we see before our very eyes? Or are such words always simply a deception in some sense?

This also becomes problematic when we stop to consider the role that the analogy of being (*analogia entis*) plays in our understanding God. The analogy of being basically states that there is a similarity between God and God's creation, at least a similarity large enough that we can use our words and representations (language) to talk about God. Yet if the only way to describe God is through our analogies, which help us to express anything at all to each other about God—but which are also always woefully inadequate to describe God's essence—how are we able to say anything about God really in the end? And how would such statements, via analogy, be able to become doctrinal statements? Wouldn't there be a greater dissimilarity between God and God's creation than a similarity, as we are contrasting something infinite with finite things?

These thoughts take us back, once again, to the contrast between positive and negative theologies. Negative theology tries to preserve the mystery of God, and not to let language overstep its limitations. Preserving the mystery that can be said to lie at the heart of religion is like preserving the mystery inherently involved in things themselves, as no word can ever fully define or exhaust the being of a thing or person. We will always use language to describe reality—the positive aspect—though we will always have to admit that the object or experience are not one and the same thing—the negative side.

Both language and religion evolve over time and both change into new forms, and are capable of being (more or less) violent in the ways they impose themselves upon us without our consent. Yet when a language changes, there will be people who refuse to admit to some changes, wanting to stick to an "original" or "pure" version of the language, or religion, despite the reality that it is being changed by those who speak it. This is evident even in those religions that uphold a certain language as itself particularly "holy": Hebrew for Jews, Arabic for Muslims, Greek for Greek Orthodox Christians, Pali for Theravada Buddhists, Sanskrit for Hindus, and Latin for Roman Catholics.

We should also consider the necessity of learning the practices and habits of someone who speaks a language or religion: both involve a "full immersion" process. This is what has led some theologians to speculate that the only way to acquire religious belief is to begin immersing oneself in its practices. As the theologian Stanley Hauerwas, for one, has contended, if you want to believe in God, you must first get down on your knees and pray to God, asking God to help you believe. Though this may sound like a circular argument, there is yet a certain truth in the sense that religion *is* a structured system of meanings and signs (with a particular vocabulary and syntax even) that can really only ever be understood by those who immerse themselves in that world and learn to "speak" the "language of faith." For so many religious persons, their "strong" faith experiences were primarily the result of being in a community where one was continuously practicing the faith because they were surrounded by those who were practicing the faith with them.

This point raises issues not only concerning how someone comes to believe *through* the practices of the faith, but also how someone can be said, if at all, to convert. You cannot simply say that you want to speak French, you must immerse yourself in French language, culture, literature, geography, and so on, before you will be able to learn to "converse" in French. Is religious conversion not little more than immersing oneself in a particular religious community and practicing their faith with them? This is all well and good, as things should be, though many questions remain about why one community is chosen over another.

This contextual deep dive might also help us to understand how a traditional statement like, "There is no salvation outside the church"—the teaching historically put forth by the church, for example, but applicable to other religions as well in one form or another—could function as truthful insofar as the word "salvation" truly doesn't have any meaning *outside of* the believers who use the term and who give it its meaning. There is no "salvation," strictly speaking, for those who do not speak this specific language of salvation.

At the same time, however, little to nothing is actually being said about the primacy of one community over another; the historical dominance of one group over another group; the limits and toleration of violence within a given community, often witnessed in how it treats its minority populations; or disputes about truth between various communities. The question that is basically left unanswered by the sheer multiplicity of existing communities, whether linguistic or religious, is what are we to do with so many options before us? Why should anyone choose a particular religious community to be a part of as opposed to any other?

The answer, as underwhelming as it may seem, is again to be found in the parallel operations of language and religion. There really isn't much of a reason to choose one over another, unless one can point to specific, concrete examples of where the community that practices the language or religion are exclusionary of particular groups or persons to the point that some within the community begin to speak prophetically to others about the levels of injustice or violence taking place in their midst.

Why someone should be Hindu as opposed to Presbyterian, or Jewish as opposed to Sikh, makes about as much sense as that one should speak German instead of Japanese, or Swahili instead of Spanish. The context in which we find ourselves—with our families, our neighbors, our schools, and our neighborhoods—says much more about why we are part of a particular religious or linguistic tradition than any truth claims each institution makes.

What both religion and language represent, in terms of truth, is that each has the capacity to describe reality in somewhat accurate, or maybe just helpful, terms. Language enables its user to provide something like a more or less truthful sketch of whatever they observe before their eyes. I can tell you, for example, about the tree I see in my front yard, how tall it seems and how its leaves change color each season, because I use language to convey these truths.

In religious terms, I can use the religious tradition's vast range of teachings and stories to convey fundamental truths about what it means to be human and what it means to face the inhumanity we sometimes exhibit to one another as well. Religion has done a splendid job of giving us a robust account of how to address grieving, how to channel one's joy, how to deal with feelings of guilt, how to characterize the misdeeds of others, how to best use our resources to aid others, and so on. The stories and traditions that make up each tradition provide a blueprint for how to go about describing and shaping one's personal and communal realities. Generally speaking, the human race has been better off because of our use of both language and religion.

But what do we do when we are faced with the plurality of languages and religions in the modern age in which we live? Do we claim that some are better than others, more capable of depicting reality, or more adept at guiding us in our day-to-day lives?

The only identity we can have is one that is developed in relation to other identities. We are interdependent beings who rely on others in order to know who we are. It may sound like a simple thing to say this, or to focus on what it means, but there are a lot of other truths that come rushing forward once we accept this most basic of premises. For example, we begin to perceive both faith and plurality a lot differently.

Faith, as I have long argued in my introductory classes where so many students these days don't want to hear about religious faith, is a relationship. In fact, if you don't like the word faith because it contains too much religious baggage, then substitute the word "relationship" and you'll be just fine. You'll also understand why it is that people say crazy things like "you need faith in your life" or "I can't imagine living a single day without my faith." When you can see how faith is really about relationship, then it makes more sense, because the "crazy" person is actually saying something closer to "everyone needs relationships in their life," and this makes a lot more sense to most of us.

I think the greatest argument to be made today as to why religious traditions are fading is simply the sheer plurality of competing religious truth claims that are currently out there. It was easier to be religious when everyone you knew in your entire world was of the same religious background. Now that one can live in a cosmopolitan city, complete with Buddhist, Jewish, and Muslim neighbors, for example, one begins to wonder if any of these traditions has a comprehensive and total grasp on the truth of our human existence, or if any one of them has a monopoly on expressing the best possible version of reality. After spending a sufficient amount of time with your diverse neighbors—followed by one's Christian teacher, Hindu yoga instructor, atheist nutritionist, and that Bahá'í clerk at the mall—you wouldn't be blamed for beginning to wonder whether any of them had a privileged access to this very ambiguous thing we call truth, though this is really quite far from the truth. Relationships exist in plural form just fine. We need different people for different things in our lives and we are capable of adjusting somewhat quickly to those who leave us and the new people who arrive in our vicinity. So why do so many people perceive the recognition of a plurality of religions in our world today as the decline of religious belief instead of its proliferation in new, and perhaps wholly unexpected, ways?

When you think about religious belief as part of this definition of faith as a relationship, you might then begin to see too how the fear of plurality that appears to usher in new doubts about religious doctrines and creeds is really a fear about opening oneself up to the multiplicity of unique individuals and their communities that surround us, from whom we mostly have nothing to fear at all. It turns out, if you take the time, that your "different" neighbors throw pretty cool parties and have charming children.

Nonetheless, these religious or nonreligious "others" haunt us without end, refusing to let us settle into a permanently fixed representation of who we are to ourselves.

We get into trouble when we assume some abstract, universal truth that doesn't actually take account of the particular people who are standing right in front of us. When we actually engage said people in conversation, authentic dialogue even, we learn more about them, but also about ourselves. And we might even be more willing to contemplate that scariest of all propositions: change. We certainly put ourselves "at risk" when we talk about the things we care about most with other people, even people who disagree with us, but no real relationship—no real faith—takes root unless we are willing to be really vulnerable with others. This is the real poverty of self that we need to pay more attention to because it is actually the only self that we have: a porous, precarious self that we often try to conceal because we are afraid of just how fragile and susceptible to external influence it is.

Maintaining a true willingness to let go of one's sense of self, one's religious faith even, in order to access a deeper truth about who one is, is the very thing that we have to aim for, though that's most likely the last thing a religious person wants to hear. Finding out after a long struggle that you are exhausted and broken isn't something to shy away from, however; it's actually the thing we should be seeking to obtain, though, for obvious reasons I shouldn't have to explain, we kind of, sort of, most likely don't want to go there.

I sometimes call this fragile self the kenotic self, which borrows a word from the Christian tradition. In Christianity, there is this wild belief that their God actually chose to weaken God's own self, so to speak, by "pouring out" God's self into human form, or as it is called in Greek, *kenosis*.

This poverty of God, as it were, is not something that only God does. Everyone is called to pick up their own cross, as Christians put it, so that they too might be crucified with their God, die with their God and become "born again" through such a kenotic process. Again, this is not a demonstration of one's strength in order to defend their God against those "vile" pagans who want to remove Christmas nativity scenes from the local town hall. It is an embrace of one's weakness so that a greater, inner strength might be demonstrated. As Paul had once put it, in deeply paradoxical terms, what appears as wise or as strong to the world is actually foolish and weak, whereas what looks like weakness and foolishness to the world is actually a sign of one's true strength and deep wisdom (1 Corinthians 1:18–31).

But, of course, someone still needs to remind many Christians, especially the politically vocal ones in my own country, about their own church's teachings.

In the nineteenth century, the Catholic theologian John Henry Newman introduced a clever distinction between the weak and strong claims of reason that is incredibly simple, but incredibly helpful to understand when discussing these matters. He argued that scientific matters make strong claims because they only use reason as their standard.[2] This is what enables a math student, for example, to work out an answer to a difficult problem, and then turn to the back of the book to find the answer. If you haven't experienced this joy or didn't know the answers were generally in the back of the book, it is delightfully refreshing to utilize the strong claims of reason, because they are, in fact, very strong and hard to refute. You can try to dispute the specific claims of a scientific discovery all you want—and religious people

2. Newman, *Fifteen Sermons.*

sometimes love doing that, as in the case of evolution or, more recently, vaccinations—but you really can't dispute how the strong claims of reason work. They are just wonderful to use, and you feel so good flexing those specific mind muscles.

On the other hand, faith engages in weak claims. Newman actually formulated the argument that faith does not utilize the obvious strong claims of reason—a point I really wish more religious people understood. Rather, faith uses "weaker" claims, which are the result of a wide plurality of factors, or what you might call an internal conversation of multiple parties taking place within one's conscience. In this sense, you don't rely simply on reason, though reason does have a stake in the game. You listen instead to all kinds of voices, including reason, experience, tradition, your family's views, your nation's views, opinions, prejudices, philosophical tomes you have read a portion of, that ethics class you once took, your neighbor's sage advice, your friend's passionate plea, the cultural context you grew up in, your economic background, predispositions that accrue from your experiences of things like age, race, and gender, and so on. When you stop to think about it, there's actually an almost infinite series of factors that are battling it out within you on a minute-by-minute basis to arrive at some sort of resolution to what it is that you actually do believe.

This may sound to the layperson like an incomprehensible amount of material to sift through just to see what it is that you believe in, but, Newman tells us, this is simply how faith works. It is also why you don't always know the moment you "come to faith," because it slowly creeps up on you, building its case beneath the surface of things until one moment you find you just simply feel it all at once. The probabilities have converged through so many of these various factors that you are pushed over the edge and you find that you just believe.

The funny thing is that it isn't just faith that works this way. Again, since we can substitute relationship for faith, we are able to see too how this is exactly how love works. Love is in fact the weakest thing there is, something that can be betrayed, withdrawn, or exposed as fake in the fraction of a second. It can be questioned, criticized, and misunderstood so easily. And yet it is also, and almost without a counterargument being produced by anyone, incredibly strong, something we are quite often willing to sacrifice so much for. We intuitively know it to be true that love is potentially the strongest force in our lives, and yet, as Newman points out, it is incredibly weak in another sense too.

The main problem we repeatedly encounter in our modern world is that people frequently make a simple category mistake in that they take the strong claims of science to be the basis for the weak claims of faith, so that we get fundamentalists combing mountain tops in Turkey looking for Noah's Ark as if one can "prove" their faith like a theorem in geometry. Newman would sadly be shaking his head in chagrin at such antics because that's not how faith works. Faith, like love, relies upon weak evidence, and it should not seek to try to produce evidence in the way that a scientist would in a laboratory. It makes everyone look bad when this category mistake is applied. It is similar to, as one philosopher has put it, asking a lover to prove their love in a law court, citing evidence of gifts given, letters written, dates paid for, and the like.[3] The more one tries to prove their love, in fact, the more we start suspecting that they really aren't in love at all. This is how I feel when I see fundamentalists trying to convince others of their faith through scientific sounding pseudo-arguments.

Both love and faith make a person vulnerable by their very nature because they rely on a vast plurality of factors that cannot be boiled down into one singular, monolithic, abstract, and universal claim. To realize this truth is to realize at the same moment why love goes hand-in-hand with suffering—a point that you can grasp logically, and even without believing in a suffering God who dies for love of humanity. Love is vulnerable in its weakness and this is precisely what allows the person who experiences love to feel empathy for others who are vulnerable or who suffer.

When we see another suffer, we instinctively move toward them out of love, in love, and through love. We find solidarity with other sufferers in allowing our love to be a vulnerable love rather than a triumphant display of one's power, might, knowledge, and wealth. These things have nothing to do with love and are more likely to be utilized by those insecure folk who are trying to protect themselves against being vulnerable in the first place—they are insulating themselves from love.

Faith speaks the language of lovers, a personal, intimate language, and not the language of scientific proof. Faith can therefore, like love, achieve certainty, but it is always a fragile but necessary certainty, as in a loving relationship.

Like love too, then, you find the unconditional, the absolute, and the universal in faith, but only by going through the conditional, the contingent, and the particular. Faith embraces what is contingent in order to eventually make the contingent necessary. This is how it works because truth is a relationship, not a proposition. Relationships are contingent, but also necessary, though the only way to experience their necessity is by first entering into

3. Latour, *Rejoicing*.

their contingency, like working up the courage to ask someone out on a date that you eventually feel is your "soulmate"—wholly contingent, but leading to what eventually feels wholly necessary. It puts the self at risk and so is the only way that faith (or love) might come about. True dialogue is about finding true friendship, and this is a space where we don't ask questions about "truth" but simply live the "truth" of the relationship itself. This is also the case with something like poetry. You don't ask if a poem is true; a lover doesn't ask if their relationship is "true."

The genre of memoir and of unfurling one's life for others is a way to bring about an intimacy between author and reader, one that, like the reading of a poem, usually does not ask us to accept or reject the story as true or as false. It asks us to resonate with it, to be intimate with it, or to cease interacting with it altogether. This is not to say that one cannot be critical of a memoir for a variety of reasons. It is only to state that when a life story is genuinely told, in as honest a manner as possible, we relate to it more through our capacities for empathy, our desires to relate and understand in order to achieve intimacy, than through our desires to defend or sustain our own identity. When we open ourselves to another's perspective, we learn to recognize how our own identities are themselves contingent and how every necessary part of who we are was not always that way. We are all as fragile as any other. This is the unique poverty of spirit that we often fail to adhere to as what blesses our fragile lives.

Seeing things this way is why we can refer to faith as a process of change. If you lose your vision of who you thought God was, or even lose sight of God altogether, that is not something to fear; it is rather the possibility of finding something new. Since humans can never understand the divine, why would this be something to fear?

Genuine faith is a discourse about relationship, and so it speaks the "language of lovers" at the same time as it applauds whatever opens the door to true intimacy. Residing in "bad faith" with oneself, and so with others, generates exclusive relationships that prohibit authentic intimacy from developing. True faith, however—and I mean this in both religious and secular senses of the word—welcomes vulnerability, precarity, and brokenness because it realizes that all of us are built upon a fragile ground, one that we cannot guarantee will remain steadfast even when we need it most. This is the nature of love, and it is a contingency that can become a necessity, but only by first acknowledging its contingency. To attempt to impose faith as a necessity that does not recognize its contingent origins, its unique access to vulnerability, is to circumvent its definition in an attempt to enclose it within an impregnable fortress and so to foreclose all possibility for critique.

The narrative arc of the religious and secular autobiographies that I have studied and written about was such that the brokenness of the personal narrative was on full display.[4] In other words, the myth of the self was called into question by the author themselves. An autobiography that strives for a unity of the self—to declare the self sovereign through its faith—is a different tale, one that I avoided researching because the philosophy they express is usually one of establishing the cohesion of one's personal myth.

This focus typically leads to an abstracted deity, the absence of Christ as a force of change, critique, and destabilization of the divine and a turn toward God's sovereign will as the force that guarantees one's own self-sovereignty. Examples of this would include Augustine's *Confessions*, Thomas Merton's *The Seven Storey Mountain*, and Lauren Winner's *Girl Meets God*.

The narratives I focused on were rather those that revealed their own mythological structure as a "lie," but without trying to construct a new sovereign myth in its place. Rather, the only task before such authors was to deconstruct their own selves, pointing out the ways in which they failed to have the faith they wanted to have, or that they had once had. Teresa of Ávila says she became a nun for the wrong reasons and introduces a critical analysis of her formation of self. Mary Karr finds faith but only through getting in touch with the vulnerability of her addiction to alcohol that fragilizes her entire self. Rachel Held Evans found her adult faith through renouncing her childhood fundamentalist faith. Dorothy Day points out the hypocrisy and piousness of her youthful faith, and then, after becoming Catholic, suggests that she will be a permanent thorn in the side of the church. Christian Wiman discusses Christ as permanent change and wonders if he really has faith in any traditional sense. He declares too that he has not found an ecclesial home.[5]

What each of these authors describes is the fracturing of the self that Paul once illustrated as the key to Christian identity, which is not as secure or sovereign as one might think. Every self dies to itself through its adherence to faith, he finds, which is a dying *with* Christ. Whatever identity one takes (e.g., male or female, slave or free person, Greek or Jew), is actually further subdivided into flesh and spirit. Whatever one thinks they are, it turns out, they are not, for every social, political, and religious identity can be

4. Dickinson, *Theology as Autobiography*.

5. Teresa of Ávila, *Life of Saint Teresa of Ávila*; Karr, *Lit*; Evans, *Evolving in Monkeytown*; Day, *Long Loneliness*; and Wiman, *My Bright Abyss*. I discuss each of these authors in more detail in my book *Theology as Autobiography*.

divided from within. So instead of claiming that he possesses the identity of a Christian that can be politically mobilized to fight against other identities, he rather acts as a Jew with the Jews and a Gentile with the Gentiles and *this* is his Christian identity.

This is one of the reasons why a good number of my students who are not religious, who identify as atheists, or as one of the "nones," have at times been pleasantly surprised by the way I present theology as a deconstruction of the self. And, of course, this should be nothing to fear for those religious persons who follow these Pauline coordinates of faith. To allow oneself to be fragilized by their experience of the loss of faith is ultimately to open the mythological self to something *beyond* itself. It is basically to suggest that one should welcome the loss of their image of God because there is no human who can attain a fixed or "correct" image of God. Whatever we believe God to be, God—or, reality, for those inclined to go the secular route—will always surpass such a human creation.

This loss is undoubtedly a good thing, but it is something that many of the faithful resist with all of their might because the recognition of this truth would fragilize the myth that they have constructed about themselves and about their religious communities. It would risk destroying the sovereign sense of self that allows one to mobilize politically, socially, religiously, and so forth.

I sometimes feel the urge to write my own story of faith, of the loss of my religious faith, but I also recognize that this is hard to do when one feels fragile in their own life. Theology has held a certain appeal to me over the years because it is the domain where the abstraction of the self that grants one sovereignty is dependent on the alleged transcendence of divine being. This pattern is replicated in patriarchal formulations where men strive to become less embodied creatures in order to maintain their sovereign sense of self.

From my youth, I was only all too aware of the hollowness of these claims, but unsure why others were not more forthcoming in their observation and critique of these dynamics. It is one of the reasons why I was drawn to feminist thought in college, and why I am still hesitant to take at face value any story of one's faith that doesn't begin with an acknowledgement of how telling a story (myth) about one's own faith may be the best way to conceal one's abstracted, sovereign existence.

If I were to tell the story of my faith, for example, I would probably begin by saying that it is difficult to be a white, American, heterosexual male because is the most abstracted existence on the planet, purposely so in order to maintain its hegemonic power over other identities. And this is precisely what is typically repressed and left unaddressed, in favor of yielding instead to abstracted claims to power. This abstracted existence is often confused with the metaphysics behind divine being, and such confusion is done on purpose to legitimate the power of men, or white persons, or Americans, and so forth.

Giving an account of myself, stringing along a consistent narrative of where I find myself today, might simply be another way to maintain such a powerful hold over others. I feel that temptation at times, especially in the voices of those who wish I could tell a tale of how I found faith, how I came to believe, how it all works out according to the familiar white, male mythology. These stories have a way of "coming together" like romantic love stories where the lovers seem fated to be together, as if by divine decree. But the New Testament is actually full of lives cut short, lives tortured, and lives that, from an all-too-human perspective, didn't end "happily ever after." And I no longer feel an allegiance to any religious narrative that could be used to dominate over another religious narrative.

Paul had tried to escape the political and religious politics of death ("necropolitics" as Achille Mbembe has described it) that lie within every racism, sexism, and anti-Semitism.[6] He had cleverly discerned that the only way to find life beyond these embodied deaths was to deal the death blow to his own sense of self, and to whatever power seemed to accrue behind it. He renounced his privilege—in this case as a Jewish leader, as a Rabbinic scholar—so that he might find in the loss of his identities a new sense of existing beyond them. He considered himself a Jew in spirit, no longer concerned about what it meant to be a Jew in the flesh and this left him without a home, but it also opened him to those others who were fragilized by life, those who were excluded from community (like the non-citizen, the religiously other, and so on).

The most truthful memoirs are, for this reason, those that come to the conclusion that finding oneself, authentically experiencing conversion as a desire to let go of one's identity, is not just a moment of embracing one's personal poverty of self, but of experiencing dis-location (Karr), de-realization (Nouwen), a shattering of the self (Wiman), and even a violence done to the self out of love (Teresa of Ávila).

For those who speak the language of lovers, intimacy is only really ever experienced in the admittance of such fragilizing experiences. When we are stripped of our social and political identities (not when they are forcibly stripped, as in cases of injustice and oppression, but when we willingly give up our privilege and the authority that comes from it), then we can

---

6. Mbembe, *Necropolitics*.

encounter one another, in genuine relationship, with no presuppositions, and with an invitation only to love, tenderness, and compassion.

Faith is an experience of dislocation, de-realization, of being shattered and of being exposed to one's own vulnerability. It is an experience of the poverty of spirit that Jesus once spoke of, and an experience that also allows one to develop a self-critical perspective that raises the autobiographical to a very important level.

This is what might enable religious persons to see that God suffers with them perhaps, not that God causes their suffering, as certain theologians have already noted. This is a position that allows some to see God within their suffering, and so too within the details of their life. It also elevates the importance of the autobiographical as it displaces the notion of an abstract deity in the clouds, pulling the strings behind every action on earth. It rather allows people to see how all actions, done with one's own hands, are bound up with God's presence in a very different way, as being co-creators with God. This is an incarnational understanding that invokes an openness to vulnerability itself that yet contains a strength. The trick is to stop defending one's worldly identities, and the wealth and comfort they provide, and to start embracing one's own poverty.

One's identity is undone as faith allows poverty to dominate the narrative one gives of one's own life. This is the division of one's already established (and so divisive) social identity. This is what allows one, paradoxically, to find a different source of strength that goes beyond any political-identitarian strength.

Community is formed when we realize together that we are all fractured selves and, in this shared weakness, that we can come together in mutual support and solidarity whether we are religious or not. Our strength lies in our recognition of our weakness, and in nothing else. This is what Paul meant when he proclaimed that he only wants to know "Christ crucified" and so rely upon neither knowledge and understanding nor upon miraculous occurrences.

Mary Karr begins her memoir *Lit* by stating that every version of her life's story that she could tell would be a lie.[7] Her starting point was that there is no way to give a wholly accurate account of one's own life. Everyone constructs a myth of their life, one that they tell to themselves in order to sustain their identity throughout time. We exist to ourselves through a mythological narrative that, more or less, conceals the truth about who

7. Karr, *Lit*, 1.

we are, conceals it from others, but also from ourselves. This is the cost of human subjectivity, and it is brought about through our existence as the linguistic animals we are.

For example, we construct memories that are selective, that omit certain details: shames and traumas, to be sure, but also the mundane and the forgettable. The cost of a functioning memory is that we must forget things in order to construct a workable narrative that we can wield socially to give others, and ourselves, a sense of who we are. We exclude certain elements in order to find stability in our identity. Communities function in the same way, offering a partial and selective account of their history in order to reinforce a given narrative of themselves. As Benedict Anderson made clear long ago, we all live in "imagined communities."[8]

There are, of course, different degrees to which one might conceal or reveal the truth about themselves. It is possible to lie about one's story, just as it is possible to tell painful truths about who one "really is." We can admit that we forget things, but that we are very open to being reminded of what has been forgotten, just as easily as we can forget things because we do not want to be reminded of our faults and failures.

The myth that we tell ourselves *about* ourselves is one we repeat so that we might be sovereign *over* ourselves. Our identity is formed through those decisions we make to exclude those parts that do not cohere with the account we want to give. We are selective, precise, willfully ignorant of what we want to displace or dismiss. This is why the entire process of forming an identity is not only exclusive but what must be done through the action of a sovereign, decisive power we wish to maintain over ourselves, as over our own stories. We must establish ourselves as sovereign (as a *self*) through such acts. This is why it is so painful when it feels as if someone else is telling our story, or when our story is "owned" by someone who is not us. This is not just a matter of artistic control, but of the conditions of one's autonomy, or self-sovereignty.

Understanding the force of the personal myths we tell ourselves can be sensed in the communal myths we tell about ourselves too, and how invested in them—both politically and religiously—we become. A myth is always personal, and, if questioned, interrogates the individual personally. If the myth we feel bound to is a collectively shared one, it can also threaten the bonds of the community to call into question one's personal myth about themselves. This is why calling one's disbelief into question, whether disbelief in some forms of evolution, or one's opposition to gay marriage, or of allowing divorce, to name but a few, is not simply a matter of taking scientific

8. Anderson, *Imagined Communities.*

findings seriously or of changing with the times; these are matters of calling an entire mythological edifice into question.

When a person removes themselves and their life story from the assertion of theological propositions regarding belief—such as the confession of faith—they do so, I would argue, in order to abstract themselves, to transcend, from the immediacy of the mythological. Faith is removed from all possibility of critique when it appears to be impossible to contaminate it with the limitations of myth. At the same time, however, what actually takes place is the purest form of myth: the belief that one's personal or communal context, with all of its biases, relative perspectives, and experiences, does not influence the establishment of one's beliefs. This is like an Evangelical church, proud of its lack of stated doctrine, ironically having a very strict code of conduct which must be followed lest you be thrown out of the church. Such beliefs thereby end up being even more severe in practice.

There are but two choices: to admit that one's life story, one's myth, impacts the formulation and expression (confession) of faith—a double confession then, both of one's own myth (one's "original sin") and one's faith—or to pretend that one's faith is not dependent in any way upon one's particular myth of their self, when in fact it is. The former reveals truth even while admitting that it is mired in a fundamental untruth (myth), disclosing the theological proposition that one can receive grace while remaining rooted in our "sinful" human existence. The latter appears entirely cloaked in grace while denying its own humanity. Such denials, as they conceal and repress the truth about our embodied existence, appear as an ultimate opening to divine grace while also being willing to deny, dismiss, and denounce what is most human about our worldly existence. This is the impetus that has grounded many religious, monastic, and puritanical renunciations of our embodied existence.

The opposite of these reflections is all-too-apparent historically: someone tries to make faith certain with facts and reason alone (fundamentalism's mistake in the modern period), which one should never try to do in a loving relationship (e.g., trying to prove that one is in love by only using facts, which kills the love); or by removing oneself from their embodied reality, trying to maintain an idealized, abstracted, transcendent life in order to mimic an abstracted, transcendent deity (e.g., as men have often done in order to maintain their power and privilege); or by basing their faith on the "rules," doctrines, and propositions of faith rather than on the way their life story reveals those vulnerabilities that resonate with the experiences of the divine (in scripture, in the lives of those who live a life of faith, etc.).

The time has come, however, to admit our lives into the theoretical, and doctrinal, arguments we make, and so to risk ourselves at the same time. This is the only way in which any semblance of truth might be accessed and maintained—as a lived and embodied reality, not as a disembodied, transcendent ideal.

CHAPTER FIVE

Haunting Our Writing

I KNOW TOO WELL what I risk when I introduce myself into my writing—especially academic essays and books—as when I place myself in conversation with other voices and search for that place from which I might experience the difficult lessons of personal integrity, coherence, and being coupled, as in all true dialogue, with another life. There is no way of escaping the reality that my personal narrative is interdependent, constantly interrupted by other narratives and other selves.

I fear the death that is the silence of an audience of the other or others who stand before me, of being dismissed from a particular discourse, which is a death that many others have faced when they chose to enter themselves into their writing through the ("over") use of the first-person pronoun and all that follows from it. I feel this risk too when I take notice of the many small deaths that rage throughout history of the marginalized voices that were never heard because they were dismissed when they chose to speak from their location, as they felt they could not do otherwise.

These small deaths recall my own fear of death and of being silenced, of not being heard. They also signal my retreat into an autonomous cocoon of solitude and the temptation to identify myself and shape my narrative in relation to something that appears to go beyond me, the conditions that have historically defined the sovereignty associated with both God and the self. But perhaps there is a way to go beyond such formulations, toward witnessing the self as substitutable, the self *as* another and so as the rebirth of the self in *another* form. In what follows, I wager that over the past half century or so multiple continental philosophers have begun to point toward a resolution to these problematics, in very profound and, especially when involving the use of "I" in their own writings, often startling ways.

It was the thought, or perhaps fear, of death that brought the philosopher Gianni Vattimo to reconsider not only his relationship to belief, and so too his Catholic roots, but also the insertion of the self, the use of the first-person pronoun, into his work. I ask myself too if this was a fear arising within him of the death of himself as author. As he expressed matters,

> Then how does religion "return"—if indeed, as it seems to me, it does return—in my-our contemporary experience? As far as I am personally concerned, I am not ashamed to say that it is related to the experience of death—of people dear to me, with whom I had planned to share a longer stretch of the journey, in some cases of persons I had always imagined would be around me when my time to pass away came, and indeed that I fancied to be lovable precisely because of their virtue (ironic affection for the world, acceptance of every living being in its limit) in rendering death itself livable and acceptable (as in a line from Hölderin "heilend, begeisternd wie du").[1]

There seems to be a convergence of fears, of the death of loved ones dear to him who will not be able to comfort him when he dies, and so also a fear of his own death, but also a fear of the entrance of his voice into his writing, of the first-person pronoun, something we cannot extricate from the possible death of the author and the fear of being dismissed once one has entered oneself into the discourse, has stood before an audience and taken a risk to be oneself in their presence. Indeed, the deaths of his loved ones and his own death circulate around the death of the author and its performance, and the only thing he can do to face this death is to insert himself, as an "I," into the text in an act perhaps unconsciously intended to subvert the other deaths:

> For a long time I woke up early to go to mass, before school, before the office, before university lectures. This book could begin thus, perhaps even punning that it concerns "la recherche du *temple* perdu." But what if I were to take the liberty not just to pun but to write in the first person? I am aware that I have never written in this way except in debates, polemics or letters to the editor. Never in essays or texts of a professional charac-ter, whether critical or philosophical. Here the question arises because the following pages take up themes from a long double interview, together with Sergio Quinzio, conducted in 1995 for

1. Vattimo, *Belief*, 22.

La Stampa by Claudio Altarocca, and there we spoke in the first person; but also because the theme of religion and faith seems to require a necessarily "personal" and "engaged writing," even though it will neither be primarily narrative nor clearly refer back to a narrating-believing I.[2]

We know that such use of the "first-person pronoun"—a phrase that can only serve to introduce formality back into the painful, self-critical awareness of the risk that he is taking in the face of death—haunts him as much as it haunts the text. It alters the relationship of the reader to the author, of the author to the text, and even perhaps the author to, in this case, himself.

This self-consciousness permeates his reflections upon the grounds for belief in his life, causing him to admit that he must bring himself, the "I," into his writing on religion and faith, though there is a tremendous discomfort in doing so. It is for this reason that he begins the book with the recognition of the "I" and he ends it there as well, as it lingers in a lengthy "postscriptum":

> The manuscript of this small book was ready at the beginning of July 1995, though it was sent to the publisher only in December of the same year. This had less to do with further elaborations and corrections I might have made than with doubts that I held for a long time over the "legitimacy" of the style I had adopted, which seemed to me, and still seems, too centred on the first person. I have decided to publish it in any case, because I am convinced that a discourse on religion, which is not merely an erudite investigation, whether historical or documentary, can only be formulated in this fashion. The suspicion with which we tend to look at this kind of writing seems to reflect the tendency, which is pervasive in our culture today, to produce religious discourses without taking on the risk of direct and personal engagement in the experiences and matters of which one speaks. This pervasive attitude may be well grounded: for example, a legitimate diffidence towards the "truth" of subjective experiences, or warranted irony towards those who speak with their hearts on their sleeves, believing that such sincerity justifies the worst trivialities or the most sickening sentimentalism. Yet by the same token, the "impersonal" tone of many discourses on religion often seems to conceal a kind of moral hypocrisy which should be unmasked or made unacceptable precisely by religious experience.[3]

2. Vattimo, *Belief*, 20.
3. Vattimo, *Belief*, 93–94.

In an effort to "unmask" such potential hypocrisy, Vattimo puts himself at risk by entering into the text, making him vulnerable to the charge that he has allowed his purely subjective experiences to bias his articulation of a more "objective" truth to which philosophy typically lays claim.

In this gesture, Vattimo's wager surprisingly resonates with the meditations on belief of the poet Christian Wiman, which levied the following pronouncement: "There is no clean intellectual coherence, no abstract ultimate meaning to be found, and if this is not recognized, then the compulsion to find such certainty becomes its own punishment. This realization is not the end of theology, but the beginning of it: trust no theory, no religious history or creed, in which the author's personal faith is not actively at risk."[4]

It had been Wiman's experience of cancer and his impending death that had spurred him to reflect upon his faith and to realize that he must put himself "at risk" by entering *himself* into the processes of theological reflection, offering us the chance to glimpse alongside him the "bright abyss" that is always occupied by the self (*My Bright Abyss* is in fact the title of his memoir). Though Wiman's reflections are caught perpetually in a tension between institutional-ecclesial affiliation and his own private experiences of faith, it is only by acknowledging the existence of this tension through recourse to his experiences that he is able to isolate and identify himself, the "I" within the larger narrative.

It is my argument in this chapter that what both Vattimo and Wiman came to realize—and what each of us has to interrogate ourselves about whenever we write on subjects that matter to us at our deepest core—is that the tensions which constitute the poles of personal identity (authority and freedom, tradition and experience, religion and spirituality, orthodoxy and heresy, among so many others) represent a philosophical paradox that gives rise to the construction of the self in the first place, what Catherine Malabou has termed the "plasticity" in relation to the self.

Plasticity, as the name implies, is what "situates itself" in the abyss between "an excess of reification and an excess of fluidification. When identity tends toward reification, the congealing of form, one can become the victim of highly rigid frameworks whose temporal solidification produces the

----

4. Wiman, *My Bright Abyss*, 75.

appearance of unmalleable substance."[5] Fluidification, which escapes definition altogether, is a spectral or messianic force that ceaselessly deconstructs our every identity, or, in her words, a "lifetime." Reification, as the name implies, tends toward a fixed and permanent state of identification and definition, becoming somewhat statuesque in its appearance, and allowing us to mistake it for a permanence that does not, in reality, exist. The problem of maintaining the "I" in this space between fluidification and reification is precisely the question of *autobiography*, the construction and maintenance of the self.

In other words, we are haunted by the "I" that lingers behind whatever we write, even if we try to efface its presence from our writing. Like Vattimo, Malabou is painfully aware of the risk that she takes in writing academically in the first person. In her words,

> The decision to write *Plasticity at the Dusk of Writing* in the first person, the decision to say "I" and to speak of my own intellectual itinerary, is not a presumptuous or narcissistic claim. I know perfectly well that people won't be interested in "me." The book must be read as a narrative, written by a fictitious subject, whose reality is of no importance. I am just trying to show how a being, in its fragile and finite mutability, can experience the materiality of existence and transform its ontological meaning. The impossibility of fleeing means first of all the impossibility of fleeing oneself.[6]

The self-conscious reference to the "first person," the tactic of distancing herself from the reader, the ultimately unknowable author who is as good as dead—each of these attempts is made to distract us from what it is that we long to know, which is ourselves and the selves of the many others who are speaking to us.

The "fictitious subject" of an unimportant reality that signals once again the death of the author, however, may not be enough to hide behind, for Malabou as for anyone, as long as we yearn for the author who cannot be known, but whom we desire unendingly and precisely to know.

The narrative of the self is always a fiction, though it is a necessary fiction nonetheless.

---

5. Malabou, *Plasticity at the Dusk of Writing*, 81.
6. Malabou, *Plasticity at the Dusk of Writing*, 81.

Between the tension of tradition and experience, as between authority and freedom, we find the "I" situated precariously. This is where the self is located, as both Malabou and Vattimo have indicated, and it is where we learn to confess the selves that we are, caught in an endless tension that cannot simply be eradicated or made whole. This was, we must be reminded, the place where Augustine too had posited himself in his *Confessions* as he placed himself in the presence of the divine, realizing that he was caught between his own experiences and a tradition that was calling him to put his life in dialogue with it. His *Confessions* became as such the cornerstone for western expressions of the self intent on examining their own location in relation to the tensions that crisscross one's biography, narrative, or life-story.

Augustine's life-story compels us still because it is centered on such tensions and their impossible resolution that we nonetheless never cease to desire. Such an impossible synthesis as the basis of the "I" becomes in fact the space of transformative and creative activity, what we generally consider as the space of personal or religious conversion.

The truth, I believe, is that any conversion is marked by its own impossibility: that we never really change despite still constantly changing. I believe this aspect of conversion is what we can isolate in Jacques Derrida's reading of Augustine's *Confessions*, originally conceived as marginal notes to another essay by Geoffrey Bennington. The work is a dialogue with Bennington, while also being a dialogue with Augustine and with Derrida himself, his past, his family, his heritage, his Jewishness, and his circumcision, among other persons and identities.

In this unique text, as with so much of his writing, Derrida is caught between what claims him—heritage, religion, tradition, language, institution, peoples, cultures—and his own experiences of the hollowness of such identities. The inevitable, messianic deconstruction of each identity brought him to reflect upon the possibility of the impossible identity, or the impossible possibility that was lodged within every constituted self. He was perpetually, therefore, caught between these poles, evading "a circumference licking me with a flame and that I try to circumvent, having never loved anything but the impossible."[7]

> No point going round in circles, for as long as the other does not know, and know in advance, as long as he will not have won back this advance at the moment of the pardon, that unique moment, the great pardon that has not yet happened in my life, indeed I am waiting for it as absolute unicity, basically the only event from now on, no point going round in circles, so long as

7. Derrida, "Circumfession," 3.

the other has not won back that advance I shall not be able to avow anything and if avowal cannot consist in declaring, making known, informing, telling the truth, which one can always do, indeed without confessing anything, without *making* truth, the other must not learn anything that he was not already in a position to know for avowal as such to begin, and this is why I am addressing myself here to God, the only one I take as a witness, without yet knowing what these sublime words mean, and this grammar, and *to*, and *witness*, and *God*, and *take*, take God, and not only do I pray, as I have never stopped doing all my life, and pray to him, but I take him here and take him as my witness, I give myself what he gives me.[8]

He waits for a "unique moment" of "absolute unicity" (granted as a form of pardon) that will enable him to avow or "make truth" through his confession to one who already knows what is to be avowed in the confession, hence the only witness he could call: God. He is well aware that one can deceive others and deceive oneself by telling the truth without actual avowal or genuine confession.[9] Significantly, Derrida conceives then of a relationship with the divine wherein he takes God as his witness to what he gives himself, which was only what was first given to him. This aporia of identity is what leads him to comprehend himself "around a single event," which is to circumscribe the event embodied in his circumcision. It is a circumcision "in which I return to myself, gather myself, cultivate and colonize hell."[10]

The construction of self that Derrida conceives is precisely one made through the autobiographical confession, suggesting something like a form of, what he will call, "theology as autobiography" that is only "interested in the depth of the bedsore, not in writing or literature, art, philosophy, science, religion or politics but only memory and heart, not even the history of the presence of the present."[11] It is entirely personal and therefore also inherently secret. It must remain unknown, even to those closest to him, even—paralleling Augustine's relationship to his mother Monica in his own *Confessions*—Derrida's own mother.

It is in this context that he recalls his mother's inquiry with others as to whether or not he believed in God, and his retorts about "my religion about which nobody understands anything" but also that "she must have known that the constancy of God in my life is called by other names, so that

8. Derrida, "Circumfession," 55–58.
9. Derrida, "Circumfession," 102.
10. Derrida, "Circumfession," 103.
11. Derrida, "Circumfession," 87.

I quite rightly pass for an atheist."[12] The quest for a label, as a definitively or provisionally closed narrative, that captures his self, for others, but also for himself, becomes an impossible one that will never register a completed sense of self, at least not an autonomous, autobiographical self. Hence, he appears as if he has no religion, no belief, no faith to speak of. This is the "open secret" of his faithless faith, or his "religion without religion."[13] In these matters he followed Emmanuel Levinas toward an identity that is only able to posit itself insofar as it also realizes that it is cancelled out at the same time, invoking for us once again the unresolvable antinomy of existence that constitutes our very selves and the impossible narratives that we construct for ourselves and for others.

This was the logic of the Spanish *Marrano* that Derrida subsequently claimed for himself as his own identity.

> I am one of those *marranes* who no longer say they are Jews even in the secret of their own hearts, not so as to be authenticated *marranes* on both sides of the public frontier, but because they doubt everything, never go to confession or give up enlightenment, whatever the cost, ready to have themselves burned, almost, at the only moment they write under the monstrous law of an impossible face-to-face.[14]

Derrida seemed to be facing the potential dissolution of his own identity, much as Augustine had once portrayed the dissolution of his identity in the presence of his God. There would be no face-to-face with the divine for the self that sought to construct its identity; there is only the identity of the *Marrano* who was not what he had once appeared to others to be.

What is it that Derrida is attempting to present us with in the revelation of his secret faith and his secret religion? Was this a denial of (religious) identity at the same time as it was an establishment of the self always caught in a particular tension? How does it parallel, as indeed it does parallel, Augustine's efforts to reconstruct himself as an autobiographical subject through the development of his will in his *Confessions*? Is Derrida's theology as autobiography a step in this same direction, or the recognition that such a step can never really be fully taken?

12. Derrida, "Circumfession," 154–55.

13. Derrida, "Circumfession," 156.

14. Derrida, "Circumfession," 170–71.

The reading of Augustine's *Confessions* subsequently developed by Jean-Luc Marion might be illuminating on precisely this point, as he contends that Augustine's personal reflections are not an autobiography, which attempts to posit the self as autonomous; it is rather a "hetero-biography."[15] As he phrases matters, "In short, it is not an *auto-* but a *hetero-biography*, my life told by me and especially to me from the point of view of an other, from close to the privileged other, God."[16] It is a heterodox "de-centering" of the self toward God "by being ex-centered from himself, a praise that comes to me from elsewhere." Hence the confession that Augustine makes, Marion contends, is one wholly beyond juridical guilt and beyond any identifications.[17]

It is a self that has been stripped of its identity, of then its self in some sense, too. It is not the establishment of a sovereign subject conceived through the construction of a will that would merge identity and desire into a single effective force. It is the loosening of the self through the recognition that it is not an entirely autonomous entity.

The foil for Augustine's *Confessions*, according to Marion, is Jean-Jacques Rousseau, whose own *Confessions* merely returns his self to himself in order to praise himself, and perhaps to absolve himself above all else.[18] It is an attempt at confessing that seeks to be entirely autonomous. Rousseau's work is hence devoid of God and truly an effort toward constructing an autobiographical account of oneself. Augustine's self, as de-centered, however, runs contrary to Rousseau and so also contrary to the Cartesian subject who strives to achieve certainty of itself.[19] "In a word, access to my Being in and through my thought, far from appropriating me to myself as for Descartes, for Saint Augustine exiles me outside of myself. I have no other *ego* besides my division itself with my *self*."[20] What remains for the Augustinian heteronomous self, then, in Marion's estimation, is that "I am this very excess of myself over *myself*."[21]

The excessive or hyperbolic self that Marion locates within Augustine's *Confessions* is predicated upon the displacement of the self, something captured practically through a moment of substitution wherein what one loves becomes substituted for one's own self. This is the logic of heteronomous selving that will become a crucial distinction for Marion, as for Augustine:

15. Marion, *In the Self's Place*, 43.
16. Marion, *In the Self's Place*, 45.
17. Marion, *In the Self's Place*, 28.
18. Marion, *In the Self's Place*, 53.
19. Marion, *In the Self's Place*, 60.
20. Marion, *In the Self's Place*, 63.
21. Marion, *In the Self's Place*, 63.

"Thus is accomplished the change of place: if I am (what, therefore) there where I love, then that becomes my *self* more interior to me than my private ego. Now what I love is named God; therefore, I find myself there. Put otherwise: God appears as the place of *self* that I want and have to become."[22]

This simple but profound "change of place" becomes the cornerstone of the de-centered self, but also what allows access to the transmigration of the other into the self through the act of love—that is, what undergirds any notion of a true *conversion*. What one wants through love becomes what one is, meaning that an O/other manages to stand in the place of the self that one has become.

> The paradox, which is marked first by the comparatives that surpass the superlatives, indicates a place that I discover neither outside me nor in me, because it finds *me* in a *self* not belonging to me but to which I belong and in which I must finally arrive. God surpasses me with his absolute alterity only inasmuch as, by the very distance that it opens, he defines what I love, therefore what identifies me in my *self*.[23]

Echoing Paul Ricoeur's lectures on *Oneself as Another*, themselves inspired by the way in which Levinas describes the process of the self being held captive by the other, Marion finds in the end that "I is an other, evidently."[24] The "change of place" that defines the moment of substitution, of one for another, of the one that I am for the other whom I love, defines the self by what stands in its place—or, more precisely, by the other who stands in the place of the self.

If we keep in mind that this reading of Augustine's *Confessions* is explicitly an attempt by Marion to read Augustine from a "nonmetaphysical point of view" which entails recognition that we cannot say "something about something," but can only say "nothing about God," we might begin to see how this particular reading of the heteronomous self is not merely an exposition of a theology as *auto*-biography, but opens a pathway toward undoing any construction of an autonomous self through what we might follow Marion in calling *hetero*-biographical writing.[25]

22. Marion, *In the Self's Place*, 97.

23. Marion, *In the Self's Place*, 97–98.

24. Marion, *In the Self's Place*, 308.

25. Marion, *In the Self's Place*, 9, 19. As Marion continues, "Hence, confession and praise truly make but one, since praising God amounts to recognizing him as such, without saying anything *about* him, therefore exactly to confessing him as such" (*In the Self's Place*, 20).

What we find when the individual is seemingly compelled to write is the struggle with language and establishing the autonomous self that many would take as characteristic of Jean-Paul Sartre's unique brand of existentialism, if it were not for his renunciation of his earlier work in his autobiographical final work. Here we witness a confession that is also, like Augustine's, a retraction of sorts, as the two are always bound together.

For Sartre, as for the characters of his many novels and plays, the construction of the self through an absolute freedom signaled an explicitly autonomous self that would rightly call to mind the importance of the autobiographical establishment of the self. But such a construction of the subject becomes undone by Sartre's own autobiography, *Les Mots*, or *The Words*, which seeks to upend his entire life's work and to reconstruct his relationship to language—his efforts to write himself into being as a subject—in order to portray another relationship to language that had been overlooked. For this reason, Sartre's autobiographical account of his early years hints toward a different sort of self and a different sort of writing (perhaps even a hetero-biography), and thereby becomes a conversion narrative akin to a religious conversion, as Philippe Lejeune has sufficiently demonstrated.[26]

What Sartre rubbed up against for most of his life was what he called the "bright unsubstantiality" of reality that the words fight against.[27] He wanted to find a substance that he could adhere to, that was already present within him, that was the material of the subject itself—and he found this material in language, in the words that somehow constructed the self as if from nothing.

> In Platonic fashion, I went from knowledge to its subject. I found more reality in the idea than in the thing because it was given to me first and because it was given as a thing. It was in books that I encountered the universe: assimilated, classified, labeled, pondered, still formidable; and I confused the disorder of my bookish experiences with the random course of real events. From that came the idealism which it took me thirty years to shake off.[28]

It is important to remember that this "disorder" of his "bookish experiences" was precisely what he confused with "real events," leaving him firmly ensconced within an idealism that would neglect the interrelationships between persons. Indeed, in his words, "At nightfall, lost in a jungle of words, jumping at the slightest sound, taking the creaking of the floor for

26. Lejeune, *On Autobiography*, 77.
27. Sartre, *Words*, 26,
28. Sartre, *Words*, 51.

interjections, I felt I was discovering language in the state of nature, without human beings."[29] Books were his religion; the library his temple.[30]

He began to establish his identity, his very self, as constituted through his ability to craft himself in words and into words. This linkage, and so too the autobiographical dimensions of the author—even the author who attempts to remove themselves from their more "objective" work—are unmistakably present in the employment of his every word: "the Universe would rise in tiers at my feet and all things would humbly beg for a name; to name the thing was both to create and take it. Without this fundamental illusion I would never have written."[31]

But, of course, such a powerful construction of the autonomous self through writing was eventually to be juxtaposed with the disenchantment of language that is easily confused with the truth: "What I have just written is false. True. Neither true nor false, like everything written about madmen, about men. I have reported the facts as accurately as my memory permitted me. But to what extent did I believe in my delirium? That's the basic question, and yet I can't tell. I realized later that we can know everything about our attachments except their force, that is, their sincerity."[32] It is at this juncture that we might relate the disenchantment of language with the death of the subject, as the self brought to life *through* language dies the moment it cannot utilize and command language to ceaselessly create itself.

In a very precise sense, his disillusionment with language—its inability to enchant his self and give it life—was of a piece with his fear of death, or with being dismissed as an author, unread and so unloved.

We witness in this regard his subsequent terror at the realization that death lurked everywhere and within every thing, and that he was to be as affected by this reality as anyone else. Indeed, the name on the tombstone in the cemetery, within his imagination, becomes potentially "transubstantiated" so that it is actually his name lying there, etched in marble or granite.[33] The idea, or the name, that he preferred to reality had allowed him to transgress his own reality and to embrace the death that lay upon another, to bring it within himself, to make it his name and to succumb to its dark powers of attachment. If words could cling to any *thing*, they could perhaps also transfer themselves to *another* thing, to *his* name and to *him*: "Caught in the trap of naming, a lion, a captain of the Second Empire, or

---

29. Sartre, *Words*, 57.

30. Sartre, *Words*, 59.

31. Sartre, *Words*, 60.

32. Sartre, *Words*, 69. See also p. 159.

33. Sartre, *Words*, 96.

a Bedouin would be brought into the dining room; they remained captive there forever, embodied in signs."[34]

Sartre testifies to his situation: the "transfiguration" undergone, "in order to be reborn, I had to write" and then become the voluminous corpus of writing itself that he produced:

> No one can forget or ignore me: I am a great fetish, tractable and terrible. My mind is in bits and pieces. All the better. Other minds take me over. People read *me*, I leap to the eye; they talk to *me*. I'm in everyone's mouth, a universal and individual language; I become a prospective curiosity in millions of gazes; to him who can love me, I step aside and disappear: I exist nowhere, at last I *am*, I'm everywhere. I'm a parasite on mankind, my blessings eat into it and force it to keep reviving my absence.[35]

The sheer force of his desires becomes, in this sense, overwhelming: he is a frightening fetish, on the borders between worlds; he is fragmented, torn asunder from himself; he is the writing that sustains his elusive, absent life, and that is the cost of being both universal and individual at once; he is a spectacle as curiosity, ethereal, everywhere and nowhere; he is a parasite existing only through humanity's willingness to read his words (as his self). In short, he had to die in order to write, to betray himself as such and to engage an "eagerness to write" that involved "a refusal to live."[36]

This death or "refusal to live" became the cost of his access to the imagination and the twisting of his "disorder" into his heightened literary powers.[37] It is no surprise that such a contortion of life into death and death into a disordered life was considered by him as a sort of sacralizing process, for it was this very process of becoming-subject through an absolute freedom that rivaled only the divine in its powers of pro-creation. As he confesses this confusion, "I thought I was devoting myself to literature, whereas I was actually taking Holy Orders. The certainty of the humblest believer became, in my case, the proud evidence of my predestination."[38] As he continues,

> I was taught Sacred History, the Gospel, and the catechism without being given the means for believing. The result was a disorder which became my particular order. There were twists and turns, a considerable transfer; removed from Catholicism,

34. Sartre, *Words*, 142.
35. Sartre, *Words*, 194–95.
36. Sartre, *Words*, 191. See also pp. 198 and 238.
37. Sartre, *Words*, 215.
38. Sartre, *Words*, 250.

the sacred was deposited in belles-lettres and the penman appeared, an *ersatz* of the Christian that I was unable to be: his
sole concern was salvation; the only purpose of his sojourn here
below was that he merit posthumous bliss by enduring ordeals
in worthy fashion. Decease was reduced to a rite of passage, and
earthly immortality was offered as a substitute for eternal life.[39]

In many ways parallel to the personal insights on display in Leo Tolstoy's
A Confession, the immortality and fame of the author was substituted for
eternal life.[40] Though Sartre was never to make the return journey toward
religious faith in any form, his confession does yield a pattern familiar to
religious confession and conversion. The recognition of his "sin" or "disorder," as he phrases it, therefore carries a significant weight in recognizing the
inverted liturgy that invested him within the world of the literary author.

> For a long time, to write was to ask Death and my masked Re-
> ligion to preserve my life from chance. I was of the Church. As
> a militant, I wanted to save myself by works; as a mystic, I at-
> tempted to reveal the silence of being by a thwarted rustling of
> words and, what was most important, I confused things with
> their names: that amounts to believing. I saw everything wrong.
> As long as the situation continued, I felt I was out of trouble.[41]

It is in this vein of personal inquiry that he confesses as well to being
Roquentin, the thinly veiled autobiographical protagonist of his *Nausea*,
and so how he "gaily demonstrated that man is impossible," while, in reality,

> I was impossible myself and differed from the others only by
> the mandate to give expression to that impossibility, which was
> thereby transfigured and became my most personal possibility,
> the object of my mission, the springboard of my glory. I was
> a prisoner of that obvious contradiction, but I did not see it, I
> saw the world through it. Fake to the marrow of my bones and
> hoodwinked, I joyfully wrote about our unhappy state. Dog-
> matic though I was, I doubted everything except that I was the
> elect of doubt. I built with one hand what I destroyed with the
> other, and I regarded anxiety as the guarantee of my security; I
> was happy.[42]

---

39. Sartre, *Words*, 249.
40. Tolstoy, *Confession and Other Religious Writings*.
41. Sartre, *Words*, 251.
42. Sartre, *Words*, 252.

This was why it is correct to depict Roquentin as an autobiographical stand-in for Sartre himself, though it is not correct to call *Les Mots* autobiographical in the same sense, for there is no effort made toward establishing an autonomous self in the same fashion. It is as if Sartre has finally prepared himself for his confession after having undergone his conversion. It has now become only a grasping of his own powerlessness and the realization that writing was no longer a weapon that awakened him, but a death of another sort.[43]

Can we still proclaim the death of the author when the author identifies his life with his writing, with the protagonist of his novel?

It is from this place alone that he is able to make the fundamental conversion, or "change of place," as Marion had put it, that defines the substitution of oneself for another. It is as such that he will conclude his memoir by considering himself not raised up or "above anyone" any longer.[44] This is the stunning climax of his conversion, and it is that which we need to unpack somewhat further.

The page that was blank to begin with is now crossed from top to bottom with tiny black characters—letters, words, commas, exclamation marks—and it's because of them the page is said to be legible. But a kind of uneasiness, a feeling close to nausea, an irresolution that stays my hand—these make me wonder: do these black marks add up to reality? The white of the paper is an artifice that's replaced the translucency of parchment and the ochre surface of clay tablets; but the ochre and the translucency and the whiteness may all possess more reality than the signs that mar them.

Was the Palestinian revolution really written on the void, an artifice superimposed on nothingness, and is the white page, and every little blank space between the words, more real than the black characters themselves? Reading between the lines is a level art; reading between the words a precipitous one. If the reality of time spent among—not with—the Palestinians resided anywhere, it would survive between all the words that claim to give an account of it. They claim to give an account of it, but in fact it buries itself, slots itself exactly into the spaces, recorded there rather than in the words that serve only to blot it out. Another way of putting it: the space between the words contains

43. Sartre, *Words*, 254.
44. Sartre, *Words*, 255.

more reality than does the time it takes to read them. Perhaps it's the same as the time, dense and real, enclosed between the characters in Hebrew.

When I said the Blacks were the characters on the white page of America, that was too easy an image: the truth really lies where I can never quite know it, in a love between two Americans of different color.

So did I fail to understand the Palestinian revolution? Yes, completely. I think I realized that when Leila advised me to go to the West Bank. I refused, because the occupied territories were only a play acted out second by second by occupied and occupier. The reality lay in involvement, fertile in hate and love; in people's daily lives; in silence, like translucency, punctuated by words and phrases.[45]

The struggle we see in Sartre was in many ways the struggle seen in the writings of Jean Genet, as well, what was perhaps *the* struggle of his entire life: his struggle with his voice as the author, the writer, the only apparently sovereign self, stretched over the void of existence who is yet seemingly capable of calling life into existence through their ability to speak and let each word bring a world into creation. But, because Genet recognizes this state of things that so frequently characterizes the act of writing, he is also curious as to what occurs on the blank space of the page, on the blank spaces of the transparent void that the paper itself is.

The words, which the author utilizes in order to establish the narrative, and so to establish the self as sovereign creator, serve as well to block the truth that speaks from the void itself: the revolutionary potential that words cover over in an attempt to articulate a dominant (even *grand*) narrative. As he concludes his introduction to his memoir *Prisoner of Love*, the reality of things lay in the everyday relationships, in daily lives, in "involvement, fertile in hate and love."[46]

The possible deceptions of the sovereign author are everywhere present: "But what if it were true that writing is a lie? What if it merely enabled us to conceal what was, and any account is, only eyewash? Without actually saying the opposite of what was, writing presents only its visible, acceptable and, so to speak, silent face, because it is incapable of really showing the other one."[47] But "showing the other one" is precisely what must be accomplished, even if their existence is marginal to "ordinary" existence. Hence, Genet's lifelong preference for those marginal to society: criminals, outcasts,

45. Genet, *Prisoner of Love*, 3.
46. Genet, *Prisoner of Love*, 3.
47. Genet, *Prisoner of Love*, 27.

the abnormal, the perverse, homosexuals, the Palestinians, the Black Panthers—anyone who was a "declared enemy" of whatever had formed itself as an identifiable entity.[48]

Indeed, the moment one became an identifiable or cohesive group, Genet was certain he would no longer stand in solidarity with them. Such a (non)position stemmed no doubt from his being a thief and prostitute in his youth that rendered him potentially "non-existent because of my own hollow non-life."[49] Whatever narrative attempted to foreclose upon itself, he resisted in principle.

This was the same desire that had diverted him from his Catholic roots and toward an unidentifiable form of paganism that "allows a pagan to approach everything, himself included, with equal respect and without undue humility. To approach and perhaps to contemplate."[50] It would be, as he would suggest, a paganism that emerges in a "call to love" that "came not from voices or things, perhaps not even from myself, but from the configuration of nature in the darkness. A daylight landscape, too, sometimes issues the order to love."[51] It was also a paganism that resonated with his experience one time on a plane to Japan when he heard the greeting "Sayonara" and felt the "thick black layer of Judaeo-Christian morality" stripped from his body "until it was left naked and white. I was amazed at my own passiveness. I was a mere witness of the operation, conscious of the well-being it produced without taking part in the process. I knew I had to be careful: the thing would only be a complete success if I didn't interfere. The relief I felt was rather a cheat. Perhaps someone else was watching me."[52]

The passiveness of his own experience was parallel to another experience he would undergo while in Palestine among revolutionary fighters, trying to understand their marginal nature and the way in which they fought for a freedom that would forever remain elusive. What he becomes witness to is the transfer or translation, the "change of place," that occurs between one of those fighters, Hamza, and himself in the eyes of Hamza's mother:

> Because he was fighting that night, I'd taken the son's place and perhaps played his part in his room and his bed. For one night and for the duration of one simple but oft-repeated act, a man older than she was herself became the mother's son. For "before she was made, I was." Though younger than I, during the

48. Genet, *Declared Enemy.*
49. Genet, *Prisoner of Love,* 149.
50. Genet, *Prisoner of Love,* 35.
51. Genet, *Prisoner of Love,* 38.
52. Genet, *Prisoner of Love,* 44.

familiar act she was my mother as well as Hamza's. It was in my own personal and portable darkness that the door of my room opened and closed. I fell asleep.[53]

This experience in Palestine is akin to his experience at another time while on public transit, when he felt as if he was equal to everyone else. The act of substitution, of one person for another, and of the de-centering nature of the experience, speaks to Genet of the sheer anonymity of human existence. It is for this reason, I would suggest, that this substitution haunts him forever after. Every time he recalls the son he sees the mother, and every time he remembers the mother, he sees the son.[54]

Their substitution, and his ability to be substituted for the son while also being older than the mother, follows his every attempt to establish himself *as* a subject, *as* an author, *as* the sovereign voice who creates characters and worlds—the very thing he has ceased to do after Sartre's penetrating study of his novels revealed perhaps too much about himself to himself.[55]

What his memoir *Prisoner of Love* presents us with is *another* Genet, one willing to allow himself to be substituted for another human being, even the most lowly among society—precisely those who are refused subjectivity and so forced to merge their contextual struggles as (auto)biographical lives with their precarious, vulnerable lives lived in search of food, shelter, basic rights, and so forth. Genet becomes therefore lost among the marginalized voices of the Black Panthers, and black Americans in general, of the Palestinians and their struggles for freedom, and of thieves, criminals, and prostitutes around the world who lurk in the dark corners, but who also find the darkness not so terrifying as to prevent the realizations of an equality that renders all humans anonymously substitutable with any other—*the revelation that had permeated Genet's consciousness so thoroughly in his experience of Hamza and his mother.

To consider this moment of substitution—perhaps we might say too *translation*, or the immanent transcendence of translation—as a connection of the possibility for the other within me (one's own potentiality) with the possibility of the other external to me is what undoes the subject and its identity. Hence, Genet's praise for the bravery and even *sanctity* of the "transsexual" person, or what today we would term "transgendered," whom, he notes, wears a halo and speaks with "saints, martyrs and criminals of both sexes, and with heroes and heroines."[56] Neither Hamza nor Genet

53. Genet, *Prisoner of Love*, 167.
54. Genet, *Prisoner of Love*, 176.
55. Sartre, *Saint Genet*.
56. Genet, *Prisoner of Love*, 150.

believed in God, but only, for the latter at least, in the sacred substitution of one for the other—what the "transsexual" symbolically carries within their own bodily being.[57]

It is in this sense that Genet's substitution for Hamza had opened up the story of his own life, at the same time as it also seemingly reduced the (sovereign) significance of his life, and their lives as well. This is not to suggest that their lives were not significant: they certainly were, though in an entirely different register. They dwelt as lives lived beyond the inscriptions of sovereign power; lives lived at the margins of society, searching for others who recognize an otherness within themselves as well.

> His mother was bound to be so diaphanous as to be almost invisible. But was it necessary *for me* to see more in her than the ruins of a life? Hadn't their love, hers and her son's, and my love for them, told me all there was to tell about myself? They'd lived through the Palestinian revolution—what more was needed? It had naturally worn them out. And since I, the author of this account, don't need them any more, their death won't affect me much, if I find out they *are* dead.[58]

Genet's sense of being an author at this point is slightly different than that of many other writers. It is an account not of a sovereign voice that cries out in order to create something from nothing, *ex nihilo*. His is not an effort to create an autonomous narrative of the self. It is rather the author as witness, as one who realizes all too well how he might have contrived his characters but looks for the moment of substitution as a transcendent translation or "change of place," of one life for another, that effectively undoes the image of author *as* creator and leaves him a passive witness to his own life unfolding through the lives of others. It is the willingness to relinquish one's possession of one's own narrative and to let it be rewritten by love for another.

His conversion, if I can call it this, is to recognize substitution as the genuine presence of sacrality, not the creation *ex nihilo* that defines the sovereign subject as author. The "author of Life," as the Christian scriptures have put it (Acts 3:15), is accessible only through the apparent loss of life (as subject, as identity) that renders every life equally substitutable for any other life—precisely what so many theologies of atonement that focus on Jesus's death on behalf of others have searched for throughout the centuries. It is this realization that allows Genet to perceive death differently, not to fear it, but to greet it as an opening toward something new.

57. Genet, *Prisoner of Love*, 352.
58. Genet, *Prisoner of Love*, 204.

It is appropriate, therefore, that Genet concludes his book in this fashion:

> After giving his name and age, a witness is supposed to say something like, "I swear to tell the whole truth . . ." Before I started to write it I'd sworn to myself to tell the truth in this book, not in any ceremony but every time a Palestinian asked me to read the beginning or other passages from it or wanted me to publish parts of it in some magazine. Legally speaking, a witness neither opposes nor serves the judges. Under French law he has sworn to tell the truth, not to tell it to the judges. He takes an oath to the public—to the court and the spectators. The witness is on his own. He speaks. The judges listen and say nothing. The witness doesn't merely answer the implicit question "how?"—in order to show the "why" he throws light on the "how," a light sometimes called artistic. The judges have never been to the places where the acts they have to judge were performed, so the witness is indispensable. But he knows a realistic description won't mean anything to anyone, including the judges, unless he adds some light and shade which only he perceived. The judges may well describe a witness as valuable. He is.
>
> What's the point of that medieval-, almost Carolingian-sounding oath in the courtroom? Perhaps it's to surround the witness with a solitude that confers on him a lightness from which he can speak the truth. For there may be three or four people present who are capable of hearing a witness.
>
> Any reality is bound to be outside me, existing in and for itself. The Palestinian revolution lives and will live only of itself. A Palestinian family, made up essentially of mother and son, were among the first people I met in Irbid. But it was somewhere else that I really found them.
>
> Perhaps inside myself. The pair made up by mother and son is to be found in France and everywhere else. Was it a light of my own that I threw on them, so that instead of being strangers whom I was observing they became a couple of my own creation? An image of my own that my penchant for daydreaming had projected on to two Palestinians, mother and son, adrift in the midst of a battle in Jordan?
>
> All I've said and written happened. But why is it that this couple is the only really profound memory I have of the Palestinian revolution?
>
> I did the best I could to understand how different this revolution was from others, and in a way I did understand it. But what will remain with me is the little house in Irbid where I slept

for one night, and fourteen years during which I tried to find out if that night ever happened.

This last page of my book is transparent.[59]

Genet's willingness to engage in substitution opens us up to another paradigm by which to consider the importance of the autobiographical self within the writings we undertake. It may sound strange to suggest, but perhaps the conclusion Giorgio Agamben's *Homo Sacer* project points to is the inclusion of a previously excluded narrative: the (auto)biographical that may serve as an "exclusive inclusion," example, paradigm or form-of-life in contrast to the "inclusive exclusion" that characterizes sacrifice and states of violent exceptionalism.[60]

This is why, in highly uncharacteristic fashion, the personal biographies of Guy Debord, Martin Heidegger, and Michel Foucault, as well as the diaries of Helen Grund Hessel, suddenly play a significant role in the conclusive study of his series, *The Use of Bodies*, the final volume wherein he asks: "What does it mean that private life accompanies us as a secret or a stowaway?" Just as quickly, he answers: "First of all, that it is separated from us as clandestine and is, at the same time, inseparable from us to the extent that, as a stowaway, it furtively shares existence with us. This split and this inseparability constantly define the status of life in our culture."[61] Every detail of daily and bodily life coexists with us at all times, though it remains conspicuously absent from the constitution of our identities.

Contrary to the Cartesian process of positing a subject, Agamben proclaims in accord with Michel Foucault's description of what it means to care for the self that "there is not a subject before the relationship with itself and the use of the self: the subject is that relationship and not one of its terms."[62] In other words, "The self is nothing other than use-of-oneself."[63] Expressing the self as a relation with its own use allows us to reconceive of the self entirely: "The user, always unauthorized, is only the *auctor*—in the Latin sense of witness—who bears testimony of the work in the very gesture in which, in contemplation, he revokes it and constantly puts it back into use."[64]

59. Genet, *Prisoner of Love*, 374–75.

60. Agamben, *Homo Sacer*.

61. Agamben, *Use of Bodies*, xx.

62. Agamben, *Use of Bodies*, 101.

63. Agamben, *Use of Bodies*, 54, de-emphasized from the original.

64. Agamben, *Use of Bodies*, 64.

But just such a passive, and perhaps hetero-biographical, *auctor* is to be contrasted with the notion of an (autobiographical) author who is the creator *ex nihilo* of a story, the one who in fact possesses what has been written rather than simply giving testimony to what has seemingly always already been written—a position that is rather one of abiding within the potentiality of the text rather than attempting to actualize it as the source of one's own (sovereign) self. Seeing things thus allows Agamben to reconsider entirely the construction of a space of intimacy and privacy where the self is actually created.[65]

The manner of constituting a philosophy or any written work that excludes one's (auto)biographical life (*bios*), at the same time as it excludes one's animal life (*zoè*), rendering "bare life" visible at the same time as it is excluded, is an exercise in the creation of a dominant self, but also an inherent and immediate self-deception, in that the self which has just been created is maintained at the cost of deceiving itself by excluding what gave rise to it in the first place. Thus, what it has truly given rise to is an active auto-immunity that Derrida once isolated as a deconstructive force within every written text, institution, or nation-state, among other normative measures.

Agamben contrasts such deception with the search for a form-of-life that renders legible another way of residing with the embodied life that one is, but which does not need to establish a sovereign self or subject as it has traditionally been understood. In his words, "With the term *form-of-life* . . . we understand a life that can never be separated from its form, a life in which it is never possible to isolate and keep distinct something like a bare life."[66]

It is a "whatever being," as he has elsewhere called it, whose singularity is not predicated on subjecting another to its dominance.[67] The divisions that characterize the split between *zoè* and *bios* within the subject—an inherent othering of the self that mirrors the othering of others within our world in myriad ways—are effaced through the institution of a form-of-life that makes visible the autobiographical details of one's life (*bios*) as well as one's vulnerability to life (*zoè*). This form-of-life lays these details bare in order to access life itself, and the lives of others as well, in ways previously not experienced at certain social levels (e.g., ethical, political, religious, and so forth).

Dwelling as a form-of-life is a "manner of rising forth," a "mode of being, which is its welling up and is continually generated by its 'manner' of being."[68] In his words, again:

65. Agamben, *Use of Bodies*, 92.
66. Agamben, *Use of Bodies*, 207.
67. Agamben, *Coming Community*.
68. Agamben, *Use of Bodies*, 224.

> Theologians distinguish between the life that we live (*vita quam vivimus*), namely the sum of facts and events that constitute our biography, and the life by means of which we live (*vita qua vivimus*), that which renders life livable and gives to it a sense and a form (it is perhaps what Victorinus calls *vitalitas*). In every existence these two lives appear divided, and yet one can say that every existence is the attempt, often unsuccessful and nevertheless insistently repeated, to realize their coincidence. Indeed, only that life is happy in which the division disappears.[69]

Mirroring the fracture between *bios* and *zoè*, there is the life that constitutes our biography and that which renders each precarious life livable. Their separation, however, is only apparent, the result of the fiction of sovereignty that establishes itself precisely through the creation of this original fracture within the constituted subject. Attempting to merge the two sides, while thereby also preserving them, is bound to fail—this is where the "form of life," as opposed to the form-of-life, is to be located. It is only when the division itself disappears, when it no longer seems relevant, that we encounter the form-of-life lived beyond the (sovereignly established) law.

This is where we can locate Agamben's fascination with Foucault's *Lives of Infamous Men* or Krafft-Ebbing's sexual biographies wherein "the life *that* has been lived is identified without remainder with the life *by which* it has been lived," as well as his interest in ancient biographical attempts to "define a life starting from a work" and so reach out toward a form-of-life.[70]

The singular life enmeshed within a singular body can only bear witness to its existence, as an almost passive subject who recognizes their own inoperativity with respect to established ("operative") normative identities (as subjects and subjectivities).[71] Striving to become a paradigmatic existence rather than a form of subjectivity, the form-of-life reaches beyond the "exclusive inclusion" that characterized bare life in order to establish an "inclusive exclusion," or what he will eventually call "an intimacy without relation."[72] The form-of-life presents us with an intimacy beyond our ability to name or identify it—like lovers showing one another their naked bodies which are otherwise normally covered over with clothing as they represent

---

69. Agamben, *Use of Bodies*, 226.

70. Agamben, *Use of Bodies*, 227–29.

71. "What we call form-of-life corresponds to this ontology of style; it names the mode in which a singularity bears witness to itself in being and being expresses itself in the singular body." Agamben, *Use of Bodies*, 233.

72. Agamben, *Use of Bodies*, 236.

the "inappropriable" or "unthinkable" that is yet the "negative foundation of politics" and, he will add, of ethics.[73]

In other words, love is expressed only insofar as we show to the other our failure to construct a consistent and cohesive narrative for ourselves.

How are we then to show this form-of-life to one another? We certainly cannot make an autobiographical claim in the sense of establishing the self through writing in order to be sovereign over ourselves and over others. There can only be something akin to the results of the hetero-biographical form that Marion introduced us to, what Agamben finds absent from most contemporary art forms, including, I would suggest, a good deal of autobiography or memoir—what contemporary art has mainly become.

In his estimation, the many forms of contemporary art have substituted "life itself for the work. But at this point, if one does not wish to remain imprisoned in a vicious circle, the problem becomes entirely paradoxical insofar as it tries to think the artist's form of life in itself, which is precisely what contemporary art attempts but does not seem to be able to achieve."[74] The highly personal, even confessional, nature of art in our world today merges with capitalist-consumerist patterns of subjectivity that would elevate celebrity as the form of glory that undergirds the sovereign self.

What Agamben is after, rather, is a form of art that is willing to become anonymous. As he puts it,

> The truth that contemporary art never manages to bring to expression is inoperativity, which it seeks at all costs to make into a work. If artistic practice is the place where one is made to feel most forcefully the urgency and, at the same time, the difficulty of the constitution of a form-of-life, that is because in it there has been preserved the experience of a relation to something that exceeds the work and operation and yet remains inseparable from it. A living being can never be defined by its work but only by its inoperativity, which is to say, by the mode in which it maintains itself in relation with a pure potential in a work and constitutes-itself as form-of-life, in which *zoè* and *bios*, life and form, private and public enter into a threshold of indifference and what is in question is no longer life or work but happiness. And the painter, the poet, the thinker—and in general, anyone who practices a *poiesis* and an activity—are not sovereign subjects of a creative operation and of a work. Rather, they are anonymous living beings who, by always rendering inoperative the works of language, of vision, of bodies, seek to

73. Agamben, *Use of Bodies*, 237–38.
74. Agamben, *Use of Bodies*, 246.

have an experience of themselves and to constitute their life as form-of-life.[75]

Contemporary art is not able to capture the inoperativity of the human being and so fails again and again to depict accurately what Sartre and Genet had both already discovered: that the artist is equal to everyone else and that only this type of anonymous living as an embrace of the forms-of-life that they uniquely are would provide the movement toward a happiness that is possible only in embracing one's inoperativity, of being then a passive witness to one's own life.

By embracing the substitution of oneself for another that renders everyone potentially equal to anyone else, there is a profound loss of the self that is also an opening to the other and a restoration of the self on another level altogether, one lived beyond the representations, laws, identities, and inscriptions that otherwise routinely identify human individuals. We can only access the space for love as an "intimacy without relations," by making use of, but not seeking to possess, our own narrative. Agamben's reflections therefore appear as a meditation upon a long line of commentary upon the autobiographical and its impossibility as an autonomous, sovereign form, providing us rather with an alternative formation of the self that considers its potential for substitution as the hallmark of its being.

75. Agamben, *Use of Bodies*, 247.

Conclusion

As DAVID TRACY HAS already noted in his book *The Analogical Imagination*, there is a ceaseless interplay at work within most discourses between those positive constructs that give us form and meaning for our identities and communities—what comes about through acts of analogical reasoning—and a type of negative dialectics that deconstructs those very same structures.[1] This tension mirrors Nietzsche's contrast between monumental and critical histories, which should be an obvious one to imagine: there are some histories that stand like statues, making monuments of the past so as to enshrine them in their own sacred aura. And then there are those critical histories that work to undo the monumental ones.[2] Though Nietzsche saw this tension at work well before his own nineteenth century, many of us are still living with the delusion that tearing down a statue because we now know more about what "really took place" in the past was an unknown occurrence before the twenty-first century.

This tension is an inescapable part of our lives though it is often not noted as a *necessary* tension that we cannot escape once and for all, try as we might. In particular, it has lain underneath a variety of historical contestations, most notably in the work I do, for example, in the field of political theology, where genealogical-deconstructivists ("radical political theologians" immersed in continental philosophical lines of thought) are typically pitted against those who would defend the analogy of being (*analogia entis*) through more orthodox and communitarian means in order to establish and defend religious identities and communities.[3]

This sounds like a very academic thing to say, and it is. But what interests me even more is how we use entire fields of thought to mask over the simplest of distinctions: sometimes we feel like we have an identity

1. Tracy, *Analogical Imagination*.
2. Nietzsche, *Untimely Meditations*.
3. See Dickinson, *Continental Philosophy and Theology*.

and we know who we are. Other times, we feel we've lost sight of it all, and everything has been taken away from us, leaving us adrift in the swell of nothingness. And, somehow, we come out of it and go back to feeling more like "ourselves," or we don't, and we plunge deeper into the abyss.

But, really, when do we become better informed about the processes themselves, the swinging between both poles that is just a part of being human? When do we get to acknowledge that some days we will feel a bit more lighthearted and other days a bit heavier of heart?

When will we let what haunts us into the light of day and acknowledge its presence, from repressed voices speaking from the margins of global academic discourses to the autobiographical self that has been kept out of "more reputable" academic writing for centuries?

From another perspective, these necessary tensions are the same ones that constitute western political thought, dividing those arguing for a liberal vision of an ever-expanding and endless egalitarianism (and which tends toward a theological pantheism at its extreme) from the sovereign decisions that institute identity and order through representational fiat (and where a more deistic portrayal of the divine is most likely to form). Theological discourse still has to come to terms with such divisions, and they are not easily, if ever, overcome.

Perhaps the entire theological project, even religion itself, must be left behind before we can look more realistically at how we sacralize things in our world—histories, persons, nations, peoples, institutions, and the like. Perhaps we need to go so far as to profane them if we are to develop better models of relating to ourselves and to one another.

Throughout this short book I have been pointing toward a possible solution, among many others I suspect, where we might begin to notice how looking directly at this tension does not mean forever overcoming it, as with the many attempts to permanently destroy metaphysics or overcome ontotheology once and for all. Rather, I have pointed toward the possibility of using dualistic thinking in ways that both acknowledge its political, economic, and social elements, while also seeking to move beyond them, though not by eradicating the dualisms, but by fulfilling them.

In this sense, much like Jesus's establishment of a hypernomian position vis-à-vis the law, we should not be attempting to permanently do away with the law (or any representation, doctrine, institution, or normative, canonical measure), but to go through it to its end so that we might reconsider, and make new use of, its presence in our world.

As Agamben has highlighted in the historical context of Franciscan debates regarding material relationships, it is the contrast between possession and use that begs us to reconsider what it might mean to make use of something rather than seek to possess it.[4] This is a point that is quite significant to consider too when contemplating what it might mean to make use of theology and religion, but not to possess them—something about which humanity has not even begun to think through the implications. This is also where we can potentially encounter the grounds for rethinking a healthier ecological worldview based on a responsible sense of usage and not of possession.

For example, I would locate one significant and meaningful site for how such divisions play themselves out in the various social and cultural contestations that linger within the tensions between established and institutionalized religious traditions and the increasing phenomena of atheism and the secular society in which we frequently live in the West. What I believe theology will need to increasingly consider is how secularism and atheism speak not necessarily from the margins of theological discourse and ecclesial communities, though they do this to be sure in some way, but from *within* the heart of Christianity's most basic claims about itself: from the death of Christ on the cross (the "crucified God"), to mystical theologies espousing a negation of negation itself (to divide the divisions that constitute our identities), which leaves its traces in the philosophical "death of God," the decline of metaphysics and ontotheology, as well as in those experiential dark nights of the soul.

What is the real challenge of atheism today? In the face of an increasingly secular society—one that seems to distrust religious faith in general—how are we to keep up something that might be called "belief in God," which has been so wedded to political and religious institutions that it becomes difficult, in an age of distrust toward authority, to know what belief *is* anymore?

There is no doubt that the typical religious atmosphere that once permeated so much of western society has slowly been eroding. You can no longer take it for granted that people are religious. Quite frankly, for many, however, this is a situation welcomed with a sigh of relief—because we had seen such "religious" people, and to be honest, they weren't always the nicest. Some religious persons had been willing to do quite a few nasty things if only they could maintain the appearance of being a good believer. Today,

---

4. Agamben, *Use of Bodies.*

you have to work harder at things; faith must be more palatable. I can't say that this is a bad thing at all. We demand more from faith, and we should.

Trying to pit "people of faith" against scientific, rational mindsets, skeptics, and atheists is a false dichotomy in many ways. If genuinely embodied, both sides in this tension are deeply complex and so intertwined with one's personal life and context that it is hard to judge either side as inadequate in a truly objective way. Negotiating the realities and complexities of living a life of belief or unbelief—whatever these things truly are—is a terribly difficult thing to do, and one that will most likely require sustained engagements with both religious and non-religious structures. Above all, an ongoing critical examination of one's personal experiences must constantly accompany any search into these waters.

Though atheism and a secular outlook in general might be seen by some to stand apart from religious claims about reality, I believe they represent only one half of a much larger picture. Atheism is the inevitable outcome of the liberal, critical-deconstructivist worldview that works from within the sovereign defenses of religious identity and doctrine, undoing their claims and offering us a profaned way of seeing the world that is not reliant upon a sacred aura to justify one's identity.

In this sense, we cannot ignore the atheist-secularist paradigm, but must find some way to incorporate it within our most fundamental, constructivist claims regarding reality, even those that are historically marked as religious. Though the religious impulse to sacralize the "natural" ways of our world will never fully recede from view, we must learn to balance such efforts with the profaning force of critical thought so that we might contemplate a more realistic vision of ourselves and our world as the complex and messy human beings that we are.

A healthy respect for a secular worldview is thus the one way to make inroads into respecting the balance that this dualistic impasse presents us with. Another can be found in the realms of interreligious and comparative thinking in general insofar as these methods divide the divisions that are perceived to lie between various religious communities and identities. In this way, they are preferred sites necessary for addressing the dualistic tensions embedded within the "sacred" discourses of our world. If religion and theology are to have any future, they will only find it by being able to establish their bearings as a fundamentally comparative inquiry, one that will undoubtedly transform much of what they had thought to be their sacred deposits of faith.

The German Lutheran pastor Dietrich Bonhoeffer once imagined the possibility of a "religionless Christianity" as he faced the reality of his own death. We are still contemplating what such a thing might resemble today. Bonhoeffer, who was implicated in a plot to kill Hitler, put into a prison camp and executed shortly before the end of the Second World War, has gone on to inspire many Christians to rethink the foundations of Christianity.

Essentially, he went from being a declared Lutheran Christian of his day to someone willing to contemplate what he termed a "religionless Christianity," as well as what Christianity, he felt, must look like in his time in order to be *effective at losing*, at least in terms of institutional "strength." His focus was on how Christians are called to be morally "strong," which is to be socially "weak," and how the names and organizations matter much less than we often consider them.

While in prison, Bonhoeffer's experiences of the religious "other," and the desperate plight of many Jews around him—something which he had not had to face prior to his incarceration—prompted him to open himself up to an experience of otherness that transcended his self-identity. He was able to dislodge his privileged status as a "true believer" despite his once having suggested that Christians are moving through this world as if sealed in a train car, untarnished by the world. He likewise began to admit that the world, and its inhabitants, many of whom were not Christian at all, affected him in ways that he had not previously anticipated:

> That misery, sorrow, poverty, loneliness, helplessness, and guilt mean something quite different in the eyes of God than according to human judgment; that God turns toward the very places from which humans turn away; that Christ was born in a stable because there was no room for him in the inn—a prisoner grasps this better than others, and for him this is truly good news. And to the extent he believes it, he knows that he has been placed within the Christian community that goes beyond the scope of all spatial and temporal limits, and the prison walls lose their significance.[5]

It was the social experiences of marginalization, imprisonment and suffering that gave him a renewed perspective on his Christian faith—one that put him in close proximity to others who now saw life similarly, though they did not share his social label of being "Christian." It was this experience that opened him up to the others around him, in their radical otherness to him—and in such a way as to later prompt him to reflect upon how Christian identity will always contain within itself a form of otherness that will

5. Bonhoeffer, *Letters and Papers from Prison*, 225–26.

defy the institutional identities that we so often cling to for security and stability.

This is a core element of Christian faith that many are loathe to admit exists, but that we cannot resist noticing if one strives to take the story of Jesus seriously.

In the modern world, we are often pushed toward living life in a certain "irreligious" state, you might say. We can no longer presume a basic religious mentality behind our culture or ourselves, at least not in the West.

Bonhoeffer's response to such a state, however, was not to try to work defensively against the tide as many have tried and are still trying to do, but rather to envision a new form of Christian identity, one that might even appear as irreligious, but which would be fundamentally focused on addressing the question of: "How can Christ become Lord of the religionless as well? Is there such a thing as a religionless Christianity?"[6] These are perhaps strange questions to many, and certainly not very easy ones to answer. Nonetheless, Bonhoeffer was moved by his experiences to contemplate the reality of trying to answer them. As he would further shape his inquiry:

> How do we talk about God—without religion, that is, without the temporally conditioned presuppositions of metaphysics, the inner life, and so on? How do we speak (or perhaps we can no longer even "speak" the way we used to) in a "worldly" way about "God"? How do we go about being "religionless-worldly" Christians, how can we be ek-klesia [in Greek font in original], those who are called out, without understanding ourselves religiously as privileged, but instead seeing ourselves as belonging wholly to the world? Christ would then no longer be the object of religion, but something else entirely, truly lord of the world. But what does that mean?[7]

I wonder about this too: what would it mean to consider Jesus as significant while not seeing the church as being as significant as others had once taken it to be. This reminds me of something Søren Kierkegaard once said in the nineteenth century about himself: I am not a Christian, but Christ is the most important thing to me in my life.

Bonhoeffer, while in prison, was being called out *from* the church by an otherness that lay beyond it, but which also drew him closer to the meaning of the "Christian" story. For him, this meant not necessarily talking about religion with the presuppositions one normally has about religious identity, but rather exploring opportunities for traditional religious claims to have a

6. Bonhoeffer, *Letters and Papers from Prison*, 363.
7. Bonhoeffer, *Letters and Papers from Prison*, 364.

new life beyond traditional religious vocabularies—ones that may overlap a great deal with secular or atheist perspectives, and therefore ones that many are scared to embrace as well. What he was also after, I think, was having to take seriously the translation of Christian terms into other languages, some of which may appear as entirely foreign or secular.[8]

What Bonhoeffer pursued was a core experience of God that might entail a certain "freedom from religion," but which would also, almost paradoxically, draw him closer to God.[9] What he realized was that such an experience might actually put him at odds with those *within* the church who had a particular way of doing things that might run counter to his new experiences:

> In these words and actions handed down to us, we sense something totally new and revolutionary, but we cannot yet grasp it and express it. This is our own fault. Our church has been fighting during these years only for its self-preservation, as if that were an end in itself. It has become incapable of bringing the word of reconciliation and redemption to humankind and to the world.[10]

This is harsh criticism perhaps; but we must also remember that there were many Christians and churches more than willing to go along with Hitler's project of National Socialism, and that such institutional allegiances must be denounced.

For true Christians, Bonhoeffer felt, ones who sought out the inner core of faith that Jesus had promulgated through his life and death, prayer and social action are what now call the Christian to existence, and these are things that need not be labeled as part of any particular social, cultural, political, or religious structure. They are simply part of one's life, and the way in which one lives it.

His focus therefore shifted in his writings from "being Christian" to simply "being human," as the humans we are in God, those who are able to embrace the suffering of the world and the many "others" who suffer. "It is not a religious act that makes someone a Christian, but rather sharing in God's suffering in the worldly life."[11] As such, he boldly claims, "The church is church only when it is there for others."[12] In other words, the church is

---

8. See Bonhoeffer, *Letters and Papers from Prison*, 390.

9. Bonhoeffer, *Letters and Papers from Prison*, 366.

10. Bonhoeffer, *Letters and Papers from Prison*, 389.

11. Bonhoeffer, *Letters and Papers from Prison*, 480.

12. Bonhoeffer, *Letters and Papers from Prison*, 503.

only the church insofar as it ceases trying to be the church and insofar as it tries to live for others.

The kenotic nature of Christianity, including seeing Christianity as the religion of the end of religion as many have put it, entails a willingness to pour itself out to the point that it no longer exists, which may just yet demonstrate its universality, but only at the cost of its existence. In many ways, this is the ultimate victory of nonviolence, as a victory over violence itself, but only at the cost of the death of the individual self-immersed in the privileges of its identity.

What lives on after the kenotic outpouring may be disregarded by those who remain, but it doesn't make the gesture any less effective. The impulse for peace and its regard for the victim is what survives and is what we carry in the modern period through the birth of human rights and a heightened concern for the marginalized.

Jean-François Lyotard had defined Christianity as the religion that potentially escapes becoming itself a grand narrative in precisely this sense, through the recognition of a kenotic love that seeks to undermine its own sovereign claims.[13] The constant, and misleading, temptation is either to defend Christianity and its formations of communal identity against a culturally threatening atheism, or to sacrifice Christianity in favor of an atheistic worldview that finds it hard to justify communal engagement of any kind. Both options must be resisted in order to reveal the true kernel of kenotic, loving weakness that is the only way of universally reaching out to one another.

What if this was what really haunted the western philosophical, theological, and literary traditions that I have been speaking about throughout? What if we learned to listen to these dynamics in ways we have not yet done?

I want to link Bonhoeffer's insights on the weakening of religious faith in the modern world to another theological illustration: that of contemporary forms of atheism and what they have to teach us about living the life of faith. I am not talking, however, about the more recent torrent of "new atheists," whom I don't think are really that exciting. To my mind, they don't confront the issue of faith from a proper perspective. In other words, they don't necessarily confront the reality of suffering and death as that which religion addresses in ways that not many other things in life do, and which is what Christianity confronts at its core. So, I want to take a look at the theology of another twentieth century German Protestant, Jürgen Moltmann, who

13. Lyotard, *Differend*.

had some interesting things to say about atheism and belief in general in the modern world.

To begin with, Moltmann doesn't see atheism and faith as being necessarily at odds with one another: "The atheism that wants to free men and women from superstition and idolatry and the Christianity that wants to lead them out of inward and outward slavery into the liberty of the coming kingdom of God—these two do not have to be antagonists. They can also work together."[14] Good critical reasoning brought to bear upon the powers of this world can be something that both worldviews share in common, and this is a point often overlooked. Likewise, he was quick to suggest that, from a Christian point of view, there is nothing to fear in the "death of God" because we have already seen God die. Or, put another way perhaps, "God overcomes God."[15]

God has a way, in the Christian narrative, of destroying one's image of God and of leaving humanity with something so vague and mysterious (i.e., the Holy Spirit) that one is hard pressed to even give it a short description. And this is why Christianity contains within itself as well, and always, a critique of religion and religious structures that we cannot overlook.[16] Such a perspective is what enables Moltmann to declare, somewhat controversially, that "Only a Christian can be a good atheist"[17]—which is to say, an atheist to the false gods that seem to appear from around every corner today, the false gods of money, of popular culture, of political leaders and systems, and even of religion in some contexts.

To suggest that "God is dead" may be one way to characterize living in our modern world, but if this is all we see—the loss of something that once gave us structure and security—then we are missing out on a major potential here. To live in the world "as if without God" means, from Moltmann's perspective, as from Bonhoeffer's, that humans are simply called to live as human beings, first and foremost, and to worry about what we call this later on, if we even do call it something at all.[18] Christians, above all else, should be able to recognize those who feel abandoned by society and by religion, as the Christian proclamation begins, and as Moltmann puts it, with the cry of Jesus on the cross of "my God, my God, why have you abandoned me?"[19]

---

14. Moltmann, *Theology of Hope*, 9.

15. Moltmann, *Theology of Hope*, 131.

16. Moltmann, *Theology of Hope*, 295.

17. Moltmann, *Crucified God*, 195.

18. Moltmann, *Theology of Hope*, 171.

19. Moltmann, *Crucified God*, x.

Christianity really becomes a form of "permanent iconoclasm," as he puts it, destroying our (always false) notions of God in order to push us toward an ever expanding vision of the divine that we can never actually complete.[20] In other words, the first people to be critical of institutional religion should be Christians (along with the full capacity of our abilities to reason), though they are often anything but this willing to critique and protest.

Jesus's death, Moltmann continues, is a "death of God," but also as a conquest of death itself and so the "death of death"—or what he calls a "negation of negation."[21] This, I would suggest, is the only legitimate path to be followed theologically today, and it is one that actually opens humanity up to otherness in a way that we have often not been willing to perceive. The Christian is called to negate the negative, and not to fight it with the construction of some positive structure that we think will win out over it.

We must enter into it and criticize it from the inside-out. We must occupy the places where it exists and go along with those who live such lives so that we might expose its limitations from *within*. If that means agreeing with much of what atheism says (though, really, what does it say?), we must go along and explore its logic from the inside-out, and not simply try to rebuff it at the borders of our fortresses of identity and institution.

This is one of the reasons that I return to these white, western, male authors as they yet refuse to immerse themselves further within the powers and privileges that characterize their lives as they were handed to them. Instead they seek to be dispossessed of their inheritance and to find other ways to access the grace and liberation that puts them closer in dialogue with others.

The atheist psychoanalyst Jacques Lacan once said, parallel to Moltmann's remarks, that it was only the theologians who could really be atheists.[22] I love this quote, and I think it is, for the most part, entirely correct. It is only those who appear to be delving into the most holy of thoughts who can really fool themselves into thinking they are much closer to truth than they really are. The rest of us, the non-theologians, have to struggle with things, with reality even—not with vague abstractions of the divine, but with concrete matters, and concrete persons.

Lacan also said, in the same context, that when love and hate meet, love lets hate win, because that's what love is, the weaker of the two—and this is how it should be. If we put these two statements together, I do not think we are very far off from where Moltmann left us, at the threshold of

20. Moltmann, *Crucified God*, 87.
21. Moltmann, *Theology of Hope*, 211.
22. Lacan, *Encore*, 45.

belief and atheism, but also favoring the weakness of love over the apparent strength of hate.

Our writings are haunted by our selves, which we often conceal in order to feign an objectivity that was never actually present, just as European philosophy is haunted by so many other global approaches to thought, and as the church is haunted by other communities that speak their truths to which we have not really listened. The time has come, the time is overdue, when we cease to speak with a fear of ghosts in our closets and start confronting those ghosts directly, welcoming them and the realities they represent before our very eyes.

Bibliography

Adorno, Theodor W. "Resignation." In *Critical Models: Interventions and Catchwords*, translated by Henry W. Pickford, 289–93. New York: Columbia University Press, 1998.

Agamben, Giorgio. *The Coming Community*. Translated by Michael Hardt. Minneapolis: University of sMinnesota Press, 1993.

———. *Homo Sacer: Sovereign Power and Bare Life*. Translated by Daniel Heller-Roazen. Stanford: Stanford University Press, 1998.

———. *The Open: Man and Animal*. Translated by Kevin Attell. Stanford: Stanford University Press, 2004.

———. *Profanations*. Translated by Jeff Fort. New York: Zone, 2007.

———. *The Time that Remains: A Commentary on the Letter to the Romans*. Translated by Patricia Dailey. Stanford: Stanford University Press, 2005.

———. *The Use of Bodies*. Translated by Adam Kotsko. Stanford: Stanford University Press, 2016.

Althaus-Reid, Marcella. *Indecent Theology: Theological Perversions in Sex, Gender and Politics*. London: Routledge, 2000.

Anderson, Benedict. *Imagined Communities: Reflections on the Origin and Spread of Nationalism*. Rev. ed. London: Verso, 2006.

Appiah, Kwame Anthony. *Cosmopolitanism: Ethics in a World of Strangers*. New York: Norton, 2007.

Aristotle. *Metaphysics*. In vol. 2 of *The Complete Works of Aristotle*, edited by Jonathan Barnes, translated by W. D. Ross, 1552–729. Princeton: Princeton University Press, 1984.

Augustine. *Confessions*. Translated by Henry Chadwick. Oxford: Oxford University Press, 1991.

Azoulay, Ariella Aïsha. *Potential History: Unlearning Imperialism*. London: Verso, 2019.

Badiou, Alain. *Saint Paul: The Foundation of Universalism*. Translated by Ray Brassier. Stanford: Stanford University Press, 2003.

Baldwin, James. "The Fire Next Time." In *Collected Essays*, edited by Toni Morrison, 291–348. New York: Library of America, 1998.

Baring, Edward. *Converts to the Real: Catholicism and the Making of Continental Philosophy*. Cambridge: Harvard University Press, 2019.

Baudrillard, Jean. *The Illusion of the End*. Translated by Chris Turner. Stanford: Stanford University Press, 1994.

Benjamin, Walter. "Critique of Violence." In vol. 1 of *Selected Writings*, edited by Marcus Bullock and Michael W. Jennings, translated by Edmund Jephcott et al., 236–52. Cambridge: Harvard University Press, 1996.

———. "On the Concept of History." In vol. 4 of *Selected Writings*, edited by Howard Eiland and Michael W. Jennings, translated by Edmund Jephcott et al., 389–400. Cambridge: Belknap, 2003.

———. "Unpacking My Library." In vol. 2, pt. 2 of *Selected Writings*, edited by Michael W. Jennings, Howard Eiland, and Gary Smith, translated by Harry Zohn, 486–93. Cambridge: Harvard University Press, 1999.

———. *Walter Benjamin's Archives: Images, Texts, Signs*. Edited by Ursula Marx et al. Translated by Esther Leslie. London: Verso, 2007.

Bhabha, Homi K. *The Location of Culture*. London: Routledge, 1994.

Boeve, Lieven. *God Interrupts History: Theology in a Time of Upheaval*. London: Continuum, 2007.

Böhme, Hartmut. *Fetishism and Culture: A Different Theory of Modernity*. Translated by Anna Galt. Berlin: De Gruyter, 2014.

Bonhoeffer, Dietrich. *Letters and Papers from Prison*. Dietrich Bonhoeffer Works 8. Edited by John W. de Gruchy. Translated by Isabel Best et al. Minneapolis: Fortress, 2009.

Bridgstock, Martin. *Beyond Belief: Skepticism, Science and the Paranormal*. Cambridge: Cambridge University Press, 2009.

Butler, Judith. *Parting Ways: Jewishness and the Critique of Zionism*. New York: Columbia University Press, 2013.

Chakrabarty, Dipesh. *Provincializing Europe: Postcolonial Thought and Historical Difference*. Princeton: Princeton University Press, 2007.

Congar, Yves. *True and False Reform in the Church*. Translated by Paul Philibert. Collegeville, MN: Liturgical, 2011.

Connolly, Tim. *Doing Philosophy Comparatively*. London: Bloomsbury, 2015.

Connolly, William. *The Ethos of Pluralization*. Minneapolis: University of Minnesota Press, 1995.

Day, Dorothy. *The Long Loneliness*. San Francisco: Harper & Row, 1981.

Derrida, Jacques. *The Beast and the Sovereign*. Edited by Michel Lisse, Marie-Louise Mallet, and Ginette Michaud. Translated by Geoffrey Bennington. Vol. 1. Chicago: University of Chicago Press, 2009.

———. "Circumfession." In *Jacques Derrida*, translated by Geoffrey Bennington. Chicago: University of Chicago Press, 1999.

———. *Monolinguism of the Other; or, The Prosthesis of Origin*. Translated by Patrick Mensah. Stanford: Stanford University Press, 1998.

———. "Sauf le nom." In *On the Name*, translated by David Wood, John P. Leavey, Jr., and Ian McLeod, 35–88. Stanford: Stanford University Press, 1995.

———. *Specters of Marx: The State of the Debt, the Work of Mourning and the New International*. Translated by Peggy Kamuf. London: Routledge, 1994.

———. "White Mythology." In *Margins of Philosophy*, translated by Alan Bass, 207–72. Chicago: University of Chicago Press, 1982.

Diamond, Jared. *Collapse: How Societies Choose to Fail or Succeed*. New York: Penguin, 2011.

Dickinson, Colby. *Between the Canon and the Messiah: The Structure of Faith in Contemporary Continental Thought*. London: Bloomsbury, 2013.

————. *Continental Philosophy and Theology*. Leiden: Brill, 2018.

————. *The Fetish of Theology: The Challenge of the Fetish-Object to Modernity*. London: Palgrave Macmillan, 2020.

————. *Theology as Autobiography: The Centrality of Confession, Relationship and Prayer to the Life of Faith*. Eugene, OR: Cascade, 2020.

————. "Whose Fetish? A Response to Prof. J. Lorand Matory, Author of *The Fetish Revisited: Marx, Freud, and the Gods Black People Make*." *The Religious Studies Project*, October 5, 2020. https://www.religiousstudiesproject.com/response/whose-fetish/.

————. *Words Fail: Theology, Poetry, and the Challenge of Representation*. New York: Fordham University Press, 2016.

Dorrien, Gary. *The Barthian Revolt in Modern Theology*. Louisville: Westminster John Knox, 2000.

Esposito, Roberto. *Persons and Things: From the Body's Point of View*. Translated by Zakiya Hanafi. Cambridge: Polity, 2015.

Evans, Rachel Held. *Evolving in Monkeytown: How a Girl Who Knew All the Answers Learned to Ask the Questions*. Grand Rapids: Zondervan, 2010.

Franke, William. *On the Universality of What Is Not: The Apophatic Turn in Critical Thinking*. Notre Dame, IN: University of Notre Dame Press, 2020.

Freud, Sigmund. *Beyond the Pleasure Principle*. Edited and translated by James Strachey. New York: Norton, 1990.

————. *Moses and Monotheism*. Translated by Katherine Jones. New York: Vintage, 1939.

Genet, Jean. *The Declared Enemy: Texts and Interviews*. Edited by Albert Dichy. Translated by Jeff Fort. Stanford: Stanford University Press, 2003.

————. *Prisoner of Love*. Translated by Barbara Bray. Middletown, CT: Wesleyan University Press, 1992.

Girard, René. *I See Satan Fall Like Lightning*. Maryknoll, NY: Orbis, 2004.

————. *Violence and the Sacred*. Translated by Patrick Gregory. Baltimore: Johns Hopkins University Press, 1977.

Girard, René, and Gianni Vattimo. *Christianity, Truth, and Weakening Faith: A Dialogue*. Edited by Pierpaolo Antonello. Translated by William McCuaig. New York: Columbia University Press, 2010.

Gordon, Avery F. *Ghostly Matters: Haunting and the Sociological Imagination*. 2nd ed. Minneapolis: University of Minnesota Press, 2008.

Guha, Ranajit. *History at the Limits of World-History*. New York: Columbia University Press, 2022.

Hauerwas, Stanley. *The Hauerwas Reader*. Durham: Duke University Press, 2001.

Hegel, G. W. F. *Science of Logic*. Translated by A. V. Miller. Atlantic Highlands, NJ: Humanities Press, 1969.

Hill, Annette. *Paranormal Media: Audiences, Spirits and Magic in Popular Culture*. London: Routledge, 2011.

Hitz, Zena. *Lost in Thought: The Hidden Pleasures of an Intellectual Life*. Princeton: Princeton University Press, 2021.

Hobbes, Thomas. *Leviathan*. Edited by Christopher Brooke. New York: Penguin, 2017.

Jameson, Frederic. *Valences of the Dialectic*. London: Verso, 2010.

John of the Cross. *The Collected Works of St. John of the Cross*. Translated by Kieran Kavanaugh and Otilio Rodriguez. Washington, DC: Institute of Carmelite Studies, 1991.

Kant, Immanuel. *Critique of Pure Reason*. Edited and translated by Paul Guyer and Allen W. Wood. Cambridge: Cambridge University Press, 1997.

Karr, Mary. *Lit*. New York: Harper, 2010.

Kierkegaard, Søren. *Attack upon "Christendom."* Translated by Walter Lowrie. Princeton: Princeton University Press, 1968.

Kripal, Jeffrey J. *Authors of the Impossible: The Paranormal and the Sacred*. Chicago: University of Chicago Press, 2010.

Kristeva, Julia. *This Incredible Need to Believe*. Translated by Beverley Bie Brahic. New York: Columbia University Press, 2009.

Lacan, Jacques. *Encore: The Seminar of Jacques Lacan: On Feminine Sexuality, the Limits of Love and Knowledge, 1972–1973*. Edited by Jacques-Alain Miller. Translated by Bruce Fink. New York: Norton, 1998.

Latour, Bruno. *Rejoicing: Or the Torments of Religious Speech*. Translated by Julie Rose. Cambridge: Polity, 2013.

———. *We Have Never Been Modern*. Translated by Catherine Porter. Cambridge: Harvard University Press, 1993.

Lejeune, Philippe. *On Autobiography*. Translated by Katherine Leary. Minneapolis: University of Minnesota Press, 1989.

Luther, Martin. *Only the Decalogue Is Eternal: Martin Luther's Complete Antinomian Theses and Disputations*. Translated by Holger Sonntag. Minneapolis: Lutheran Press, 2008.

Lyotard, Jean-François. *The Differend: Phrases in Dispute*. Translated by Georges Van Den Abbeele. Minneapolis: University of Minnesota Press, 1988.

MacIntyre, Alasdair. *Whose Justice? Which Rationality?* Notre Dame, IN: University of Notre Dame Press, 1988.

Malabou, Catherine. *Plasticity at the Dusk of Writing: Dialectic, Destruction, Deconstruction*. Translated by Carolyn Shread. New York: Columbia University Press, 2012.

Marion, Jean-Luc. *In the Self's Place: The Approach of Saint Augustine*. Translated by Jeffrey L. Kosky. Stanford: Stanford University Press, 2012.

Matory, J. Lorand. *The Fetish Revisited: Marx, Freud, and the Gods Black People Make*. Durham: Duke University Press, 2018.

Mbembe, Achille. *Critique of Black Reason*. Translated by Laurent Dubois. Durham: Duke University Press, 2017.

———. *Necropolitics*. Durham: Duke University Press, 2019.

McGowan, Todd. *Universality and Identity Politics*. New York: Columbia University Press, 2020.

Metz, Johann Baptist. *Faith in History and Society: Toward a Practical Fundamental Theology*. Translated by J. Matthew Ashley. New York: Crossroad, 2007.

Moltmann, Jürgen. *The Crucified God: The Cross of Christ as the Foundation and Criticism of Christian Theology*. Translated by R. A. Wilson and John Bowden. Minneapolis: Fortress, 1993.

———. *Theology of Hope: On the Ground and the Implications of a Christian Eschatology*. Translated by James W. Leitch. Minneapolis: Fortress, 1993.

Moore, R. I. *The War on Heresy*. Cambridge: Belknap, 2014.

Nancy, Jean-Luc. *Dis-enclosure: The Deconstruction of Christianity*. Translated by Bettina Bergo, Gabriel Malenfant, and Michael B. Smith. New York: Fordham University Press, 2008.

Newman, John Henry. *An Essay on the Development of Christian Doctrine*. Notre Dame, IN: University of Notre Dame Press, 1994.

———. *Fifteen Sermons Preached before the University of Oxford between A.D. 1826 and 1843*. 3rd ed. Notre Dame, IN: University of Notre Dame Press, 1997.

Nietzsche, Friedrich. *Untimely Meditations*. Edited by Daniel Breazeale. Translated by R. J. Hollingdale. Cambridge: Cambridge University Press, 1997.

Ochieng, Omedi. *The Intellectual Imagination: Knowledge and Aesthetics in North Atlantic and African Philosophy*. Notre Dame, IN: University of Notre Dame Press, 2018.

Oliver, Kelly. *The Colonization of Psychic Space*. Minneapolis: University of Minnesota Press, 2004.

Pessoa, Fernando. *The Book of Disquiet*. Translated by Richard Zenith. New York: Penguin, 2002.

Raschke, Carl. *Force of God: Political Theology and the Crisis of Liberal Democracy*. New York: Columbia University Press, 2015.

Ricoeur, Paul. *Memory, History, Forgetting*. Translated by Kathleen Blamey and David Pellauer. Chicago: University of Chicago Press, 2004.

———. *On Translation*. Translated by Eileen Brennan. London: Routledge, 2006.

———. *The Symbolism of Evil*. Translated by Emerson Buchanan. Boston: Beacon, 1967.

Rieff, David. *In Praise of Forgetting: Historical Memory and Its Ironies*. New Haven: Yale University Press, 2017.

Ruether, Rosemary Radford. *The Church Against Itself: An Inquiry into the Conditions of Historical Existence for the Eschatological Community*. New York: Herder & Herder, 1967.

Ryle, Gilbert. *The Concept of Mind*. London: Routledge, 2009.

Sagan, Carl. *The Demon-Haunted World: Science as a Candle in the Dark*. New York: Ballantine, 1996.

———. *The Varieties of Scientific Experience: A Personal View of the Search for God*. Edited by Ann Druyan. London: Penguin, 2007.

Said, Edward W. *Culture and Imperialism*. New York: Vintage, 1994.

———. *Freud and the Non-European*. London: Verso, 2014.

———. *Power, Politics, and Culture: Interviews with Edward W. Said*. Edited by Gauri Viswanathan. New York: Vintage, 2002.

Sandoval, Chela. *Methodology of the Oppressed*. Minneapolis: University of Minnesota Press, 2000.

Santner, Eric L. *On Creaturely Life: Rilke, Benjamin, Sebald*. Chicago: University of Chicago Press, 2006.

———. *Untying Things Together: Philosophy, Literature, and a Life in Theory*. Chicago: University of Chicago Press, 2022.

Sarr, Felwine. *Afrotopia*. Translated by Drew S. Burk. Minneapolis: University of Minnesota Press, 2020.

Sartre, Jean-Paul. *Saint Genet: Actor and Martyr*. Translated by Bernard Frechtman. Minneapolis: University of Minnesota Press, 2012.

———. *The Words: The Autobiography of Jean-Paul Sartre*. Translated by Bernard Frechtman. New York: Vintage, 1981.

Siedentop, Larry. *Inventing the Individual: The Origins of Western Liberalism*. Cambridge: Belknap, 2017.

Stepanova, Maria. *In Memory of Memory*. Translated by Sasha Dugdale. New York: New Directions, 2021.

Stewart, Susan. *The Ruins Lesson: Meaning and Material in Western Culture*. Chicago: University of Chicago Press, 2021.

Stiegler, Bernard. *The Age of Disruption: Technology and Madness in Computational Capitalism*. Translated by Daniel Ross. Cambridge: Polity, 2019.

Tanner, Grafton. *The Hours Have Lost Their Clocks: The Politics of Nostalgia*. London: Repeater, 2021.

Taubes, Jacob. *The Political Theology of Paul*. Translated by Dana Hollander. Stanford: Stanford University Press, 2003.

Taylor, Mark Lewis. *The Theological and the Political: On the Weight of the World*. Minneapolis: Fortress, 2011.

Teresa of Ávila, *The Life of Saint Teresa of Ávila by Herself*. Edited by J. M. Cohen. New York: Penguin, 1957.

Tolstoy, Leo. *A Confession and Other Religious Writings*. New York: Penguin, 1988.

Tracy, David. *The Analogical Imagination: Christ, Theology, and the Culture of Pluralism*. London: SCM, 1981.

Vattimo, Gianni. *After Christianity*. Translated by Luca D'Isanto. New York: Columbia University Press, 2002.

———. *Belief*. Translated by Luca D'Isanto and David Webb. Stanford: Stanford University Press, 1999.

Warren, Calvin L. *Ontological Terror: Blackness, Nihilism, and Emancipation*. Durham: Duke University Press, 2018.

Wilderson, Frank B. *Afropessimism*. New York: Liveright, 2021.

Wiman, Christian. *My Bright Abyss*. New York: Farrar, Straus and Giroux, 2013.

Winter, Sarah. *Freud and the Institution of Psychoanalytic Knowledge*. Stanford: Stanford University Press, 1999.

Wolfson, Elliot R. *Open Secret: Postmessianic Messianism and the Mystical Revision of Menahem Mendel Schneerson*. New York: Columbia University Press, 2009.

Yerushalmi, Yosef Hayim. *Freud's Moses: Judaism Terminable and Interminable*. New Haven: Yale University Press, 1991.

Yountae, An. *The Decolonial Abyss: Mysticism and Cosmopolitics from the Ruins*. New York: Fordham University Press, 2016.

Zartaloudis, Thanos. *Giorgio Agamben: Power, Law and the Uses of Criticism*. London: Routledge, 2010.

Zinn, Howard. *A People's History of the United States*. New York: Harper, 2015.

Žižek, Slavoj. *Less Than Nothing: Hegel and the Shadow of Dialectical Materialism*. London: Verso, 2013.

Zuckerman, Phil. *What It Means to Be Moral: Why Religion Is Not Necessary for Living an Ethical Life*. Berkeley, CA: Counterpoint, 2020.

Index

Printed in the USA
CPSIA information can be obtained
at www.ICGtesting.com
LVHW022042110824
787948LV00005B/593

9 781666 769210